T0326411

Sensory and aroma marketing

Sensory and aroma marketing

edited by: Esther Sendra and Ángel A. Carbonell-Barrachina

Wageningen Academic
P u b l i s h e r s

EAN: 9789086862986
e-EAN: 9789086868414
ISBN: 978-90-8686-298-6
e-ISBN: 978-90-8686-841-4
DOI: 10.3920/978-90-8686-841-4

First published, 2017

© Wageningen Academic Publishers
The Netherlands, 2017

Wageningen Academic Publishers,
P.O. Box 220, 6700 AE Wageningen,
the Netherlands,
www.WageningenAcademic.com
copyright@WageningenAcademic.com

This book has been co-funded by the Erasmus+ programme of the European Union 'Food Quality & Consumer Studies' (Strategic partnership Erasmus + Nr. 2014-1-SK01-KA203-000464).

The European Commission support for the production of this publication does not constitute an endorsement of the contents which reflects the views only of the authors, and the Commission cannot be held responsible for any use which may be made of the information contained therein.

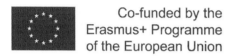 

Book reviewers:

Miroslava Kačániová

Slovak University of Agriculture in Nitra, Slovak Republic

Simona Kunová

Slovak University of Agriculture in Nitra, Slovak Republic

Table of contents

Preface

This book is based on qualified contributions of experts in the field of marketing, consumer studies, sensory analysis of foods and new technologies used in food retailing, services and marketing communication. All the chapters are outcomes of international project cooperation within Erasmus + Strategic partnership project 'Food Quality & Consumer Studies'. This project started in 2014 with the aim to modernize and improve the quality of university education in the field of food science, food marketing and consumer studies, applied through the synergic effect of international cooperation, transfer of innovation and creation of new values in project consortium of 10 partners from 9 EU countries.

Project in the form of international mobility and training activities as well as through transfer of knowledge and creation of new values has created a framework and conditions for the development and pilot implementation of 8 intellectual outputs focused on sensory studies, sensory and aroma marketing, neuromarketing for food retailing, augmented reality for food marketers and consumers, health, nutrition, food consumer trends and product development. Intellectual outcomes in three cases represent not only innovative, but an entirely new product in the field of education, which has not been used in the educational process at partner universities so far (aroma and sensory marketing, neuromarketing for food retailing, augmented reality for food marketers).

I believe that this book 'Sensory and aroma marketing' will provide readers from academic community and business sphere (university students, scholars, professionals) with theoretical and practical knowledge necessary for an in-depth understanding of sensory marketing issues at the level of theory and practical implications for food sector. Besides, even if you are not an expert in the field, you will enjoy reading the book and learning new things about how the human senses are used in sensory marketing.

Publishing of the book has been co-funded by the Erasmus+ programme of the European Union 'Food Quality & Consumer Studies' (Nr. 2014-1-SK01-KA203-000464). I would like to thank all project team members working intensively during project period (2014-2017), especially authors of different chapters, reviewers as well as all those who in any way contributed to the content, or formal aspect of the book.

Esther Sendra and Ángel A. Carbonell-Barrachina
Book editors

Elena Horská
Project coordinator

1. Introduction to sensory marketing

V. Vietoris

Slovak University of Agriculture, Faculty of Biotechnology and Food Science, Department of Storing and Processing of Plant Products, Tr. A. Hlinku 2, 949 76 Nitra, Slovak Republic; vladimir.vietoris@uniag.sk

Abstract

Everything around us is perceived by the human senses. People are able to perceive their surroundings, including market or shopping environment through sight, hearing, touch, smell, and taste. Often senses play an important role in the selection and preference of a popular product. This introduction chapter tries to describe how the human senses (sight, hearing, smell, taste, touch) play a role in the buying behaviours and how they are affected by the information gathered by our senses.

Keywords: human senses, customer's perception, behaviour, multisensory communication

Esther Sendra and Ángel A. Carbonell-Barrachina (eds.) **Sensory and aroma marketing**
DOI 10.3920/978-90-8686-841-4_1, © Wageningen Academic Publishers 2017

1.1 Introduction

Human senses play a very important role in the selection of products, and until recently senses have been underused in marketing strategies. The information that a person receives is obtained from the surrounding environment through the five human senses, the sense organs. The human organs (eyes, ears, nose, mouth, and skin), function as receptors, they are sensitive to various stimuli from the outer environment, and have specific functions. Senses allow us to see, hear, smell, taste, feel or register, and also perceive texture or temperature. The notion of human senses includes just those five senses: sight, smell, taste, touch, and hearing (Vietoris, 2008; Watts, 1989). However, there are also comprehensive multisensory stimuli, as well as other sensors, such as the proprioceptive system, which informs us about the position of the body or the muscle apparatus by which we recognize the weigh when we lift some stuff. In this introduction chapter, the author will describe the five basic senses and their role in customer decision and their application in sensory marketing.

The market environment is full of sensory stimuli; from the very pleasant to those that warn people of the danger ahead. This chapter will focus primarily on the various senses, or a combination of them, to help the consumer evaluating the situation when its senses are interacting with a product or service. Sensory receptors are necessary for an effective communication with the surrounding environment, as sensors are used to obtain the necessary information to take proper decisions. Manufacturers, who offer products and services, try to take advantage of this fact; through sensory stimuli, they try to induce appeal to customers and to convince them to buy. The relationship between manufacturers and customers is displayed in Figure 1.1.

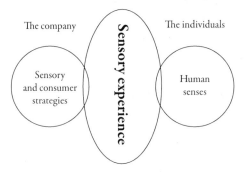

Figure 1.1. Entities interactions in sensory marketing.

1.2 Sense of sight

Now and due to an excessive use of visual stimuli, visual saturation occurs in marketing, and makes very difficult to effectively deliver a specific visual message

(Vietoris)

The most important sense in choice decisions is sight, because approximately 70% of the information we get comes from the vision. Equally important is to obtain relevant information by reading the words. The customer can then choose products on the basis of the communicated visual cues. Without a doubt, the most important part of visual communication is played by colour and psychology. For example, it is obvious that a red ripe vegetal product will be tastier and sweeter than a green unripe one. Thus, the different colours communicate different emotions, associations, moods, and specific atmospheres. The colours have the ability to influence the perception of time, which can be used, for example, in the waiting room at the doctor office or hospital. According to several authors (Mendlikova, 2011; Nestrstova, 2013), the colours are perceived through the eye receptors; they are perceived by their intensity (rods) and colour combination of red, green and blue cones. However, it is possible to deceive the eyes with optical illusions, and, therefore, marketers use these interactions. Thus, it can be easily understood the importance of visual cues, and the wide use of these stimuli in marketing. However, at present, given the over use of visual stimuli, visual saturation occurs, and makes very difficult to deliver a specific visual message effectively. In this scenario, visual stimuli used in marketing are becoming more selective for target people, and still, they offer a myriad of choices to individuals (Saidl, 2011).

Vision is the most widely used sense in sensory marketing, because it comes first and it is the activator of multisensory sensations. The choice of colour, form and shape of the product, perceived through the sense of sight, is a key factor in the entire marketing communication. Colours have a big influence on the human mind. Through the colours, customers could identify and distinguish among products, change the customer different moods, and create links to favourite products. Proper choice of light atmosphere and colouring can be a very effective first step in the salutation of the potential customers. Many studies show that the perception of colour in the in-store communication has enormous potential. But it is necessary to choose the right colour combinations and fit them to the aim of the communication (Zachar, 2008b). Through a proper selection of the colour, it is possible, for instance, to create appetite and increase hunger. With another colour combination, the perception of the waiting time in point-of-sales can be shorten. Brands and companies are also perceived through colour, by using distinctive logos, for instance. The light is just as important as the colour of the product because it completes the purchase: its diversity can be achieved playing with the source of light and its intensity. A properly selected ambient light increases the impression of being at home and willing to spend more time in the store. On the contrary, intense and artificial light supports a fast dynamics of shopping (Zachar, 2011). As already mentioned, vision is important in the food industry, where it appropriately informs the consumer, primarily on the quality of the product, and also on the quality of the environment. The sight activates the adrenal gland, and, thus, it is also the activator of the attraction to certain foods, by activating the taste buds (Mendlikova, 2011).

The primary colours can be divided into cold and warm ones. There is also a breakdown of colours into female and male colour types. Warm colours (red, orange and yellow) are perceived as colours having high energy. Red colour is considered to be a highly exciting one, stimulates the appetite and is the most attractive to human eyes, including printed material. Physiologically, the vision of the red colour increases heart rate and heart activity, and it remains in the human memory for the longest time. For example, red is the most used colour in bars and restaurants. The orange colour has similar, but slightly less intense properties as the red colour has, and it is especially popular among teenagers and children. The yellow colour is soothing, lively, cheerful, but also delicious and creamy in conjunction with food, or sour and bitter as a lemon. Warm colours are used in creative professions, where it is necessary to highlight the dynamism and energy (energy, transport, and creative advertising agencies, and media).

By contrast, cool colours (green, blue, and purple) are considered to be the colours of damping. They are used in sectors such as advocacy, conservative banking sectors, and the pharmaceutical industry. It is necessary to remember that colours have different meanings in different cultures (white means sorrow in Japan). On the basis of neuromarketing research, it has been found that the brain works the same way in all individuals, regardless of its origin (Krupka, 2007). Application and communication of the colour is specific domain of culture and the historical development of the nation. In some countries, it is good to know the meaning of colours, for example, some Eastern nations perceive the white colour as the mourning one. Marketing communication for colours, therefore, should be selected by historical consequences to create real and wanted emotions (Mendlikova, 2011).

1.3 Sense of hearing

The sounds will activate the emotional part of the human brain, thus, it is possible to use it as a tool of communication to influence the unconscious desires of the customer

(Mendlikova, 2011)

Hearing is a frequently used sense in marketing but its potential is not fully exploited. Auditory perception represents approximately 12% of the human perception (including sight, smell, taste, and touch), and 50% of sound stimuli is perceived subconsciously. The sound is a physical phenomenon and causes physical changes in the body. The sounds will activate the emotional part of the human brain, thus, it is possible to use it as a tool of communication to influence the unconscious desires of the customer. It may, therefore, be the real determining factor in consumer behaviour (Mendlikova, 2011).

The most common use of hearing is related to oral or written messages: the attention drawn to the selection of phrases, words, and voice, which are supposed to sell the information. Experimentally, it was found that voice in combination with nonverbal communications, movements, and gestures that catches the eye gets the highest attention (55% of cases), followed by the vocal melody, modulation, and voice tone (38%), and the smallest attention is paid to the content of the communication (7%). If the visual information is not considered, the audio is almost 5 times more important than the content. The second major area of audio communication is completing the atmosphere of the environment with ambient music or sounds associated with the brand. The sounds are a powerful tool for triggering the emotions and feelings that can affect the mood of the customers. In the past, music was often used for its therapeutic effects and still finds application in a variety of types of therapy, psychiatry, paediatrics and child psychiatry. When listening to music, both cerebral hemispheres are activated and release endorphins, and subsequently give rise to the feeling of satisfaction. Music and other sounds, for example jingles, are equally immediate and have a fast effect on brand recognition and emotion. A jingle creates a relatively quick impulse of communication by itself. Many companies have already created their own acoustic identity (Bačuvčík, 2008), for example Microsoft Windows, in its start-up and shutdown.

Music can be used to induce an atmosphere that can affect the movement through the store (Milliman, 1982, 1986; North and Hardgreaves, 1996). Then, good music, or sounds can affect the well-being of the customer and staff, and the perception of a product or consumer behaviour when waiting besides a point-of-sale. Studies have shown that the pace or rhythm of the music affects consumers perception of time in the stores, and their spending. A fast paced music reduces spent in shopping malls, but on the contrary, it increases the turnover of the undertakings in the food courts; this is, people eat and drink faster. On the other hand, a slow music pace leads to longer time spent in restaurants, and at the same time to increase the average spent by 29%. Differences in consumer behaviour can also be found between classical and popular music, and between known and unknown songs. The volume level is also important; loud music in a supermarket leads customers to spend less time there, and they have tendency to leave. Loud music, by contrast, is used in bars and leads to increased drinks consumption. Women tolerate less loud music than men. Buying spaces without music are generally perceived as rather negative and customers spend less time there. In rooms with music being played, customers are willing to wait longer and increase their willingness to remain in the laborious and boring environments. However, music that customers do not like can be demotivating and arise negative emotions (Boček *et al.,* 2009).

Important aspects of music are also colour and rhythm. The most basic rhythm of the life of an individual is the heart beat. Based on these two parameters (colour, rhythm), you can build the emotions and the atmosphere of the environment. For example, blue music (slow, long, calm tones) rhythmically moves below the frequency of heart beat and has a calming effect, while red music (fast, high beats per minute, drums) moves above the frequency of the heart and is more emotional; the latest (red one) is used for example in fashion shops for teenagers (Bačuvčík, 2008). As an example of the importance of audio, the company IBM launched in the 1970's the silent typewriters. As a result, customers were not satisfied and complained. Then the company electronically added sound to the new version of typewriters; the 'repaired' version of the typewriter succeeded. Auditory cues play an important role as well on the perception of food quality, as an example, Kellogg's food company success strongly relies on the sound of their breakfast cereals. There are also a number of marketing strategies including sound effects in the automotive industry: sound of opening-closing of the car, patented typical roar of motorbikes (e.g. Harley Davidson) (Mendlikova, 2011).

Some international companies are able to use different music based on local demographics and ethnic profiles to hit the target. However, if the composition of the target group is diverse, music accepted by the average population should be used. It can be concluded that the selection of music (sound support) is as important as the selection of visual elements and should correspond with the identity of the brand (Agapito *et al.,* 2012).

1.4 Sense of touch

> Consumers are happy to touch the products and want to test the product by themselves. Ingenious use of tactile cues, can be a challenge for many companies
>
> (Vietoris)

Tactile stimuli are received through the nerve endings, which are located on our skin (Cicero, 2009). Consumers receive information about the structure of the surface, temperature, and shapes of an object through their sense of touch. Right behind vision and hearing, the sense of touch remains as the most important sense for the handling of objects. However, the sense of touch has been scarcely used in marketing strategies despite the fact that consumers relate the texture experience of a product with the product itself and the brand (Mendlikova, 2011). The sense of touch is of major relevance when selecting some products, such as clothing and cosmetics. When purchasing several foods, such as fruits and vegetables, to determine the quality of the products, consumers often scan freshness by touch. For many food products, the main limiting factor for the touch sense is the protective packaging of the product; however, in many other cases, food safety recommendations advice against touching the food. In general, marketing does not pay enough attention to the texture, as assessed by touch, while this sensory attribute has a great potential. Marketing communication may have the possibility to involve the knowledge of psychology on the relation among colours and perceived properties of a material (structure, hardness/ softness). In this way, the present knowledge states that (Saidl, 2011):

▸ Hard and smooth materials (e.g. metal) represent properties such as cold, tough, and discipline, which correspond to the blue and the white area of the colour spectrum.
▸ Hard materials with structure (e.g. stone) connect with properties such as awareness, power, and compactness. In this case it is appropriate to choose the yellow area of the colour spectrum.
▸ Materials with medium hardness and structure (e.g. wood) evoke a sense of well-being, health, honesty, wisdom, and experience. They connect with the green area of the colour spectrum.
▸ Soft materials (e.g. felt, rug) represent the individuality, sensuality, alternative understandings and they are associated with red area colour spectrum.

The sense of touch may also be used to evaluate the product package or presentation, and not only the product, for example food: the wine contained in a bottle with a cork or with a twist-off cap are perceived by consumers as having different flavours. As much as 59% of consumers prefer to drink from a glass bottle compared to a plastic one or an aluminium can. A beautiful example is the multisensory bottle of Coca-Cola, which extends several sensations at the same time. Alternatively, the shape of a product may connect with the brand, as the Toblerone chocolate bar with its triangular shape, or potato chips Pringles packaged in a tube. It is possible to argue that each product has a potential opportunity to engage tactile stimuli to its identity. Consumers are happy to touch the products and want to test the product by themselves. Ingenious use of tactile cues can be a challenge for many companies.

1.5 Sense of smell

> Smell is the second most used sense, behind sight, because each person has unique and individual experiences with odours and connects them with personal experiences
>
> (Vietoris)

Olfactory cues are obtained through the human olfactory system. Smell is directly linked with human emotions. Breathing is an essential function of our daily life and an individual takes breath approximately 23,000 times daily. Together with the air, odour (perception of volatile compounds with the food outside the mouth) and aroma (perception of volatile compounds with the food inside the mouth) molecules are inhaled (Vietoris, 2008; Zachar, 2008a). Such odour and aroma molecules are recognized by olfactory cells and the information reaches the brain creating specific emotions and experiences. The primary purpose of the sense of smell is partly to warn against possible danger. Scientific studies (Lindström, 2005) showed that 75% of our emotions are created by using the smell. Our smell memory is the most intense of all the senses, and only about 20% of smell sensations are forgotten; thus, humans keep even very old memories and feelings connected to smell (Lindström, 2005).

From a marketing point of view, smell is the second most used sense, mainly in food industry marketing strategies (restaurants, fast-food service, and coffee shops). According to previous research (Berčík et. al., 2016; Zachar, 2008b), a pleasant scent can affect consumers' perception) of time, but also their visual and taste perceptions (Bradford and Desrochers, 2009; Levy et al., 2012) or create general friendly environment for customers (Kardes et al., 2014; Tarczydło, 2014).

Each person has unique and individual experiences with odours and connects them with personal experiences. Then, from the positive or negative experience with odours, positive or negative memories and links are created. The sense of smell is usually combined with taste for the evaluation of food products (Kemp et al., 2011). Intentional odour may be released into the shop to create positive buying environment: to enhance shopping intention, or to extent the shopping time (Berčík et al., 2016). Scientific evidences indicate that average people can distinguish between approximately 4,000 smell stimuli. Due to the fact that breathing is an autonomous process, it is possible to use scents to reach out everyone. Nowadays, flavourings and scents play an important role in marketing strategies (Saidl, 2011). Odorous incentives are transmitted straight into the centre of the limbic brain. This centre is the hub of both emotional (arise emotions here) and long-term memories; this explains the strong link between odours, emotions and memories. In practice, it is possible to use this evidence to influence and promote certain feelings (Mendlikova, 2011).

For instance, to create a dynamic environment, full of energy and provoking, an aphrodisiac scent (heavy flowery, deep fruity) can be used. This is particularly suitable for bars, cosmetic and jewellery shops. Peppered and natural aromas stimulate the feeling of health. On the contrary, when it is necessary to create an environment of trust, the smell of cloves is considered as the most appropriate (Zachar, 2011). Many studies evaluated the effect of applying flavourings in a store environment, and found that selling of product increased by 14.8 to 15.9%, the time spent in shop was also extended by 18.8% and also increased the interest and willingness to communicate about the bought products. All these factors lead to an increase in sales and the satisfaction degree of the customers (Mendlikova, 2011).

Today's use of smell as a marketing tool can be divided into three fields of application. The first one is the smell of the product itself; for example, the Cadillac Automobile Company uses its own aroma 'Nuances' in their cars. The second field is the use of scent in retail chains and stores. The purpose is to create a specific experience with the brand, increase brand recognition and influence buying behaviour. It has been showed that the willingness of customers to make a purchase rises when using the proper scent. On the other hand, the smell of fresh bread in a supermarket brings a serious problem: the customer feels its smell and most definitely will buy it, but then, it keeps the customer away from buying other goods or reduces their willingness to buy them (Mendlikova, 2011). This reduction in their willingness to buy is due to the fact that its sensory perception and emotions are, to some extent, satisfied by purchasing the bread. The third and last field of application of scents is their use in promotional items and media. Embedding scents in magazines, flyers, or direct mail is very convenient. Nowadays, aroma marketing is effectively used by the automotive and aerospace industry, all kinds of shops, hotels, catering halls, premises or means of transport. Some restrictions to aroma marketing are: required cautions to avoid allergic reactions due to specific scent compounds, the need to develop an individual approach to fit the experience with flavours and to take into consideration national/cultural differences regarding aroma preferences. In spite of the above mentioned considerations, aromas and scents play a very essential role in current marketing strategies.

1.6 Sense of taste

The relevance of food taste in buying decisions is limited. This is a perfect opportunity and taste can represent a great potential for creative marketing campaigns

(Vietoris)

Taste stimuli are the last sensory stimuli perceived during eating, and its perception is influenced by all other senses (sight, touch, sound, and smell) (Stone *et al.*, 2012; Vietoris *et al.*, 2008). Taste is related to food composition, but scientific evidences proved that taste perception is highly modified by other factors. As an example the taste of a drink is perceived as different if it comes from a plastic bottle or from a glass one (Zachar, 2011). Many taste studies are carried out by the food industry; however, the relevance of food taste in buying decisions is limited by the natural consumption of food and beverages. Taste and odour are closely related, both can be linked to certain memories and emotions and may be used in marketing strategies and not only by the food industry. Several studies point out that the perception of flavours may be affected by the association between taste and colour, as follows: sweet-red, sour-green, bitter-blue, and salty-yellow (Mendlikova, 2011). Combining colours and tastes may create unforgettable experiences and effective feeling of specific brands. In practice, the first filter for purchasing a food is the visual impression, and if the product is not accepted by the consumers' sight, there is no chance to taste it. To effectively reach the customer, it is, therefore, necessary to deliver visually attractive products (Lindström, 2005).

As already mentioned, thanks to synaesthesia (the interaction of senses) taste is under significant influence of other senses rather than taste receptors. If the colour of food is changed, it is much harder for consumers to associate the food with the right ingredients, typical taste, and brand. Case studies (Zachar, 2008a) even indicate that it has been difficult to recognize and differentiate blindfolded red and white wine. The most common use of taste in marketing is sensory analysis: consumer tastings as well as sampling under controlled conditions. In some cases, it is necessary to show the entire preparation of the dish and engage consumers through memorable marketing, 'show cooking' performances are getting popular in sales events (Mendlikova, 2011). In the case of non-food products, the use of flavouring substances as incentives for shopping is more difficult; however, they are commonly used on cosmetic products, such as lip glosses, lipsticks, lip balms or toothpaste. Whereas for other applications flavours use offer serious restrictions, despite the attempts made by some companies, for example iMac with their fruity colours of computers (Van Jaarsveld, 2010). Taste can represent a great potential for creative marketing campaigns.

1.7 Multisensory communication

As already mentioned, people acquire a lot of information regarding foods, especially through vision and hearing; most advertisements and billboards are communicated through these means. The fact that advertising appeals in particular to eyesight and hearing had as a consequence that people become immune to visual and auditory stimuli. It is, therefore, necessary to involve other senses as well, and their combination is needed to create new incentives, which are easier to remember by the customer. Smell and taste have not led customers to immunity yet. Combination of flavour and sound is under-rated (Spence, 2013, 2015). The use of multisensory communication can be distinguished from common competition strategies, or influence the individuals through emotional pathways, to create a positive experience and come back to it repeatedly (Mendlikova, 2011). The complexity of sensory experience is presented in Figure 1.2.

1.8 Conclusions

Sensory marketing is a very interesting way to reach consumers; widening the spectrum of purchase motivations, sensory and aroma marketing can stimulate sensory stimuli and build a relationship between the brand and the consumer. Sight and visual stimuli have been very well applied in this field and have been used for many years. However, there may be a sort of immunity to the visual perception of consumers. Aroma (smell) is also known and a very popular form of sensory marketing in business premises. Other forms of use of the senses

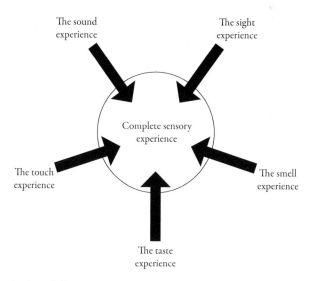

Figure 1.2. Complexity of the sensory experience.

(taste, touch and hearing) are rather marginal. Therefore, there are big opportunities opened for companies thinking about using these three senses and the related stimuli in improving the flavour and texture of new products.

References

Agapito, D., Valle, P. and Mendes, J., 2012. Sensory marketing and tourist experiences. In: Spatial and organizational dynamics discussions papers. University of Algarve, Faro, Portugal, pp. 7-18.

Bačuvčík, R., 2008. Hudba v marketingové komunikaci. Available at: http://www.bacuvcik.com/hudmk.

Berčík, J., Paluchová, J., Vietoris, V. and Horská, E., 2016. Placing of aroma compounds by food sales promotion in chosen service business. Potravinárstvo Journal 10(1): 672-679.

Boček, M., Jesensky, D. and Krofiánová, D., 2009. POP in-store komunikace v praxi: trendy a nástroje marketingu v místě prodeje. Grada Publishing, Praha, Czech Republic, pp. 224.

Bradford, K.D. and Desrochers, D.M., 2009. The use of scents to influence consumers: the sense of using scents to make cents. Journal of Business Ethics 90(2): 141-153.

Cicero, S., 2009. The sense of touch. Available at: http://tinyurl.com/mmojl2y.

Kardes, F.R., Cronley, M.L. and Cline, T.W., 2014. Consumer behaviour, 2nd edition. South-Western College Pub, Cincinnati, OH, USA, 576 pp.

Kemp, S., Hollowood, T. and Hort, J., 2011. Sensory evaluation: a practical handbook. John Wiley and Sons, Chichester, UK, 208 pp.

Krupka, J., 2007. Neuromarketing i v Česku. Lidové noviny 20(236): 16.

Levy, M., Weitz, A.B. and Grewal, D., 2012. Retail management. McGraw-Hill, New York, NY, USA, 675 pp.

Lindström, M., 2005. Brand sense: build powerful brands through touch, taste, smell, sight, and sound. Free press, New York, NY, USA, 256 pp.

Mendlikova, P., 2011. Smyslový a emoční marketing. PhD-thesis, VŠE Prague, Czech Republic, 106 pp.

Milliman, R., 1982. Using background music to affect the behavior of supermarket shoppers. Journal of Marketing 46: 86-91.

Milliman, R.E., 1986. The influence of background music on the behavior of restaurant patrons. Journal of Consumer Research 13(2): 286-289.

Nesrstová, Z., 2013. Creation of marketing communication in medical facility. PhD-thesis, Masaryk University, Brno, Czech Republic, 110 pp.

North, A.C. and Hargreaves, D.J., 1996. The effects of music on responses to a dining area. Journal of Environmental Psychology 16: 55-64.

Saidl, J., 2011. Pět smyslu, jeden nákupní zážitek. POPAI Publishing, Prague, Czech Republic. Available at: http://tinyurl.com/kt7229a.

Spence, C., 2013. Multisensory flavour perception. Current Biology 23(9): pR365-R369.

Spence, C., 2015. Eating with our ears: assessing the importance of the sounds of consumption on our perception and enjoyment of multisensory flavour experiences. Flavour 4(3).

Stone, H., Bleibaum R. and Thomas, H.A., 2012. Sensory evaluation practices. Academic Press, Amsterdam, the Netherlands, 438 pp.

Tarczydło, B., 2014. Scents and elements of aroma marketing in building of an appropriate brand image. Knowledge economy society – Managing organizations: concepts and their appliacations. Cracow University of Economics, Cracow, Poland, 378 pp.

Van Jaarsveld, K., 2010. The effect of the senses on the perception of a brand. PhD-thesis, Stellenbosch University, Stellenbosch, South-Africa, pp. 218.

Vietoris, V., 2008. Sensory analysis of food. Slovak University of Agriculture, Nitra, Slovak Republic, 75 pp.

Watts, B.M., Ylimaki, G.L., Jeffery, L.E. and Elias, L.G., 1989. Basic sensory methods for food evaluation. IDRC, Ottawa, ON, Canada, 160 pp.

Zachar, M., 2008a. Smyslový marketing-1. The image of the audit. Presentation, internal material, Prague, Czech Republic.

Zachar, M., 2008b. Smyslový marketing-2. The image of the audit. Presentation, internal material, Prague, Czech Republic.

Zachar, M., 2011. The importance of sensory marketing in the IN-STORE communication II. POPAI, Internal material, Prague, Czech Republic.

2. The sense of smell

J. Paluchová*, J. Berčík and E. Horská

Slovak University of Agriculture, Faculty of Economics and Management, Department of Marketing and Trade, Tr. A. Hlinku 2, 949 76, Nitra, Slovakia; johana.paluchova@gmail.com

Abstract

Nowadays, consumer is more sensitive and it is really appreciable seen in daily purchasing decisions. People do not remember what they saw or heard; it is only a feeling what remained in them. Smell is an important aspect of survival for humans, shown in the fact that people take prompt action after an odour stimulus. It also plays an important role in sexual selection, emotional responses, and forming preferences for food and drink. Smell is more likely to evoke emotion and memory than the other senses. There are around 1000 types of receptor cells in the nasal cavity, and people can distinguish around 20,000 different smells; thus, the ratio smells to receptor is ~20:1. It is scientifically proven that the information that is perceived by smell, affects directly and immediately the consumers' decision. In the last years, many researches have shown that sensory marketing has intensive impact on total sale of goods or services and on company' profits too. Sensory marketing is one of the marketing trends, thanks to it, it is possible to stimulate customer to purchase products and to stimulate employees to have higher activity too. The meaning of aroma marketing is increased by the fact that 75% of emotions are generated because of the smell and the human brain remembers 35% of what is felt. This chapter is a summary of how the smell sense works through odour perception and its impact on consumer emotions and purchase decision. Smell and memory are close terms and their relationship is explained. Either in a laboratory or in real conditions, air quality has to be respected and adapted for research and for spending time in each store. The final subchapter describes the historical background of aroma marketing, its practical examples, and its importance on the market, including multisensory experience in connection to scent marketing.

Keywords: air quality, aroma marketing, human emotion, olfactory bulb

2.1 How smell works

> Smell is the sense which is linked to the emotional centre of the brain. It is so powerful that it can literally force people to change their heart rate and direct their thoughts to pleasant moments in their life
>
> (Pajonk and Plevová, 2015)

When we inhale with every breath, particulates are send up through our nostrils, pass the cilia that wave them along, and are directed into the olfactory bulb, which delivers them without further ado, into our brains. If we experience a familiar or highly evocative scent, the full memory of first contact ignites both amygdala and hippocampus. In evolutionary terms, it is a little surprise that prey smells very well the hunter but predator smells no so well the prey. The sense of smell was critical to the species' survival. In the early days of medicine, smells allowed for the diagnosis of some diseases: diabetes smelled like sweet, for instance, and measles like feathers. By far, the best smellers are four-legged mammals; humans have 5 million olfactory cells, while sheepdogs have 220 million (Pradeep, 2010). Olfaction is especially important for food selection too. Much of what we call 'taste' or 'flavour' is really the odour of the food. Try holding your nose while eating, and notice how much flavour you lose. Olfaction also plays an important, easily overlooked role in social behaviour. If you were exposed to the smells of other people (without any other information about them), and you rated their desirability as a potential partner. Research has shown that our body odour, produced by the genes which make up our immune system, can help us subconsciously choose our partners (Havlicek and Roberts, 2009). Women generally show this tendency more strongly than men do (Herz and Inzlicht, 2002). Although the receptors sensitive to a particular chemical are scattered haphazardly in the nose, their axons find their way to the same target cells in the olfactory bulb, in a way that chemicals of similar smell excite neighbouring areas, and chemicals of different smell excite more separated areas (Uchida *et al.*, 2000). Then, the olfactory bulb sends axons to the olfactory area of the cerebral cortex. A complex substance, such as a food, activates a scattered population of cells (Lin *et al.*, 2006; Rennaker *et al.*, 2007). The human nose can distinguish over 10,000 different odours, being the most sensitive of the senses; besides, it has a tremendous evocative power of memories and experiences over the years (Lindström, 2010). Nef (1998) wrote that the olfactory receptors are vulnerable to damage because they are exposed to the air. Unlike receptors for vision and hearing, which remain the same for a lifetime, an olfactory receptor has an average survival time of just over a month. At that point, a stem cell matures into a new olfactory cell in the same location as the first, and expresses the same receptor protein. Its axon, then, has to find its way to the correct target in the olfactory bulb. Each olfactory neuron axon contains copies of its olfactory receptor protein, which uses like an identification card to find its correct partner (Barnea *et al.*, 2004; Strotmann and Levai *et al.*, 2004). However, if the entire olfactory surface is damaged at once, for instance, by a blast of toxic fumes, so that the system has to replace all the receptors at the same time, many of them fail to make the correct connections, and olfactory experience does not fully recover (Iwema *et al.,* 2004).

Other research helps to explain why the unusual scent worked better. The brains process first-time smells in a different way than familiar ones. The special processing, which can associate the smell with a pleasant or unpleasant experience, is unique to sense of smell (Dooley, 2012). Odours are initially registered by receptor cells in the nasal cavity. These send electrical impulses along dedicated pathways to the olfactory bulb. The olfactory bulb is part of the brain's limbic system, the seat of emotions, desires, and instincts, which is why smells can trigger strong emotional reactions. Once processed by the olfactory bulb, data is transmitted via three olfactory pathways to higher centres in the brain that process it in different ways. This process is called 'orthonasal' smelling, in which smell data travels along pathways directly from the nose. In retro-nasal smelling, odours also have a flavour component that enters the olfactory pathways *via* the mouth (Carter *et al.,* 2014). A specific smell will activate a specific pattern or array across the receptors, so that each smell has its own signature. When the receptors forming a specific pattern are activated, this signature is sent to the brain for processing (Carter *et al.,* 2014). It is generally believed that the human smell sense has atrophied in relation to other senses, but recent research shows that humans can still effectively track a scent. Using both nostrils to sample a smell, the human brain uses both sets of data to accurately pinpoint the location of the source of the odour. Therefore, with vision and hearing, smell can be stereoscopic, relying on both nostrils for a full understanding of a scent. 'Blind' smell refers to the ability of the brain to detect a smell without being consciously aware of it, which has been demonstrated in experiments using fMRI (functional magnetic resonance imaging) scans showing how olfactory areas are activated without the participant's knowledge (Carter *et al.,* 2014). Smell, the strongest trigger of emotions after sight, is for a person too important because this sense is subject of frequent reviews, suggests a study conducted in Paderborn (Neumann, 2011). This study pointed out that smell affected customer' opinion about the goods (for 85% of customers), thanks to that, the willingness to buy fragrance rose by 14.8%, the amount of time spent in the shop rose also 15%, and the general interest and willingness to communicate odour rose 19% (Neumann, 2011). Smell is a chemical sense, which is closely linked to the emotional centre of the brain and odour perception can easily navigate to the purchase of certain goods (Sikela, 2014).

In the world, there are many studies that use neuroimaging and biometric techniques in an attempt to demonstrate the impact of odours on brain activity (Lorig, 2000; Pinto *et al.,* 2014), which analysed the reactions of people after their exposure to certain fragrances using EEG (electroencephalography) signal. This is an electrophysiological monitoring method to record electrical activity of the brain, as well as exploring the impact of scents on emotions in terms of mood and physiology (Warrenburg, 2005). This examination has been extended for physical well-being and for performance in the presence of simulated ambient odours (Knasko *et al.,* 1990). Facts and myths about aromatherapy, olfactory analysis of the effects on mood, physiology and behaviour were also examined (Herz and Inzlich, 2002). Detailed knowledge of the brain processes as a response to odour impact was evaluated in a study with fMRI conducted under realistic conditions (McGlone *et al.,* 2013). It should be pointed out that almost no study has considered the factor of the air quality in the environment and its effects on the preference changes, e.g. the weather, and almost all of the studies are limited to laboratory conditions. NeuroFocus Advisory Board member, Gerald Zaltman, noted that 'Olfactory cues are hardwired into the brain ́s limbic system, the seat of emotion, and stimulate vivid recollections'. Once a scent is embedded in an individual's brain, even visual cues can cause it to be resurrected and even experienced. Zaltam sees scents shoring up marketing efforts in several ways (Pradeep, 2010). They can be memory markers that help a person recall familiar brands. They can also change the way we process information; for example, a lemon aroma can make us more alert. Zaltman speculates that scents of that type could be helpful when introducing a new product. Now with EEG testing, researchers can help determining which smell work best in which environment (Pradeep, 2010).

Pleasant and unpleasant odours provoke different autonomic reactions: skin conductance (SC), heart rate (HR), and startle reflex and are affected by odour pleasantness. Moreover, an experiment using olfactory evoked potentials has suggested differential cerebral processing of pleasant vs unpleasant odours. Functional magnetic resonance imaging and positron emission tomography-scan studies found that pleasant and unpleasant odours activate different respective neural networks. Differences in the processing of pleasant vs unpleasant odours have also been shown by using response times. Subjects had to perform four tasks: detection, intensity, hedonic, and familiarity judgments. It was shown that unpleasant odours were processed significantly faster than pleasant and neutral ones only during hedonic judgment (Bensafi *et al.,* 2002).

2.2 Smell perception and its impact on consumer' emotions

> Just thinking on the aroma of freshly ground coffee makes you immediately
> want to have a cup of coffee on your desk ready to be enjoyed

Every other sensory system must follow a long and winding path to the brain, full of transfers and hand-offs. But smell is mainlined directly into centres for emotion and memory. While 60% of human brain is devoted to sight, a scant 1% is devoted to smell (Pradeep, 2010). Olfaction, the sense of smell, is the response to chemicals that contact the membranes inside the nose (Kalat, 2014). On average, women detect odours more readily than men, and the brain responses to odours are stronger in women. Those differences occur at all ages and in all cultures that have been tested so far (Doty *et al.*, 1985; Yousem *et al.*, 1999). In addition, if people repeatedly attend to some faint odour, young adult women gradually become more and more sensitive to it, until they can detect it in concentrations one ten thousandth of what they could at the start (Dalton *et al.*, 2002); however, men, girls before puberty, and women after menopause do not show that effect, so it apparently depends on female hormones (Kalat, 2014).

Specialized receptors in the nasal cavity detect incoming molecules, which enter the nose suspended on air currents and bind to receptor cells. Sniffing sucks up more odour molecules into the nose, allowing humans to sample a smell. It is a reflex action that occurs when a smell attracts attention, and can help warn of danger, such as smoke from a fire or rotting food. Olfactory receptors located high up in the nasal cavity send electrical impulses to the olfactory bulb, in the limbic area of the brain, for processing. Table 2.1 shows examples of the worst smells in the world. The distinctive smell of the durian fruit is perceived by some as revolting but others find it extremely tempting (Carter *et al.*, 2014).

Table 2.1. The six worst smells in the world (data retrieved from Carter *et al.*, 2014).

Smell	Description
Decaying flesh	Repulsive to most people; may evoke thoughts of death
Skunk odour	Horrible to most, but a few people find it 'interesting'
Vomit	Often associated with illness, which may heighten disgust
Faeces or urine	Caused by gas released as bacteria break down food residue
Decaying food	Triggers an adaptive response to food that could cause illness
Isonitriles	Chemicals in nonlethal weapons described as world's worst smell

2.3 The secret to scent memories

> Tell me and I will forget, show me and I will understand, make me smell and
> I will remember
>
> (Chinese proverb)

People perceive the world around with the five senses and smell is just one them, but an important one because the average person can normally distinguish about 10,000 smells. On average, each person breathes 20,000 times a day and with each breath comes a chance to pitch a product because the sense of smell cannot be turned off. It is scientifically established that two people never feel the same scent despite of the fact that they are exposed to the same substance. The aroma is very different from all other sensations, because the smell of the past can unleash a torrent of memories that are sometimes so intense that it may seem as real. This type of memory is called the 'Proustian memory effect', which is named after Marcel Proust (Sikela, 2014). The special memory system for senses, for thinks that man remembers, is called 'episodic memory'. People have many other memory systems: procedural, semantic, short-term, and long-term. But, episodic memory is the function that may best be described as a mental time machine that stores memories about what, where, and when. This system is younger and more complex than other memory systems, and is mostly developed in human beings. The episodic memory system is usually not mature until a child has reached roughly the age of five; not until then the child can recall events and at the same time relate them to particular places and times. To evoke powerful memories, choose the scents of childhood: warm grass after a summer rain, cinnamon, and the salty ocean air. While humans generate the most lasting visual or audio memories between the ages of 15 and 30, the more powerful smell memories are a pony ride straight back to childhood. Studies have consistently found that human' peak smelling ability ranges from 5 to 10 years old. During those years, we have the opportunity to experience many smells for the first time, and the luxury of time to enjoy them (Pradeep, 2010).

The neurons responsible for smell are the olfactory cells, which line in the olfactory epithelium in the rear of the nasal air passages (Figure 2.1). Like metabotropic neurotransmitter receptors, each of these proteins traverses the cell membrane seven times and responds to a chemical outside the cell by triggering changes in a G-protein inside the cell. The G-protein, then, provokes chemical activities that lead to an action potential. The best estimate is that humans have several hundreds of olfactory receptor proteins, whereas rats and mice have about thousand types (Zhang and Firestein, 2002). Humans have only three kinds of cones and five kinds of taste receptors, so researchers were surprised to find so many kinds of olfactory receptors. Each olfactory receptor responds to only few stimuli. The response of one receptor might mean a fatty acid with a straight chain of three to five carbon atoms.

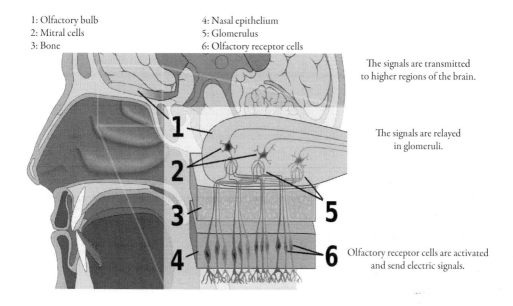

1: Olfactory bulb
2: Mitral cells
3: Bone
4: Nasal epithelium
5: Glomerulus
6: Olfactory receptor cells

The signals are transmitted to higher regions of the brain.

The signals are relayed in glomeruli.

Olfactory receptor cells are activated and send electric signals.

Figure 2.1. Olfactory receptors (image retrieved from www.scienceinschool.org/it/content/dal-metionale-al-pollo-fritto).

The response of another might mean either a fatty acid or an aldehyde with a straight chain of five to seven carbon atoms. The combined activity of those two receptors identifies a chemical precisely (Araneda *et al.*, 2000; Imamura *et al.*, 1992).

The scent and memory do not have to be related to be effective (Figure 2.1); in this case, the brut smell had nothing to do with molecular biology. The consistency of the scent was the key factor in stimulating the memory of the subjects. People will remember more about a product, even its ad copy, if it is scented. If a product is unexpectedly scented and competitive products are not, people will remember not just the scent but their opinion about the aroma of the product (Dooley, 2012). There is still much more to be learned about the relationship between chemical structure and smell. Smells are often produced by a combination of many different smell molecules and categories. Comparisons of the structures of smell molecules within each category have shown some similarities (Figure 2.1), for example, minty smelling compounds often share a similar molecular structure. Octane, a linear hydrocarbon, smells like oranges, while octanoic acid, a saturated fatty acid, which differs from octane by only one oxygen atom, smells like sweat. Re-experiencing any of the sight, smell, or sound inputs may trigger a memory of the event, but smell seems most strongly associated with memory. This experimental fact may be because olfactory regions are linked to all emotional areas in the limbic system (Figure 2.2).

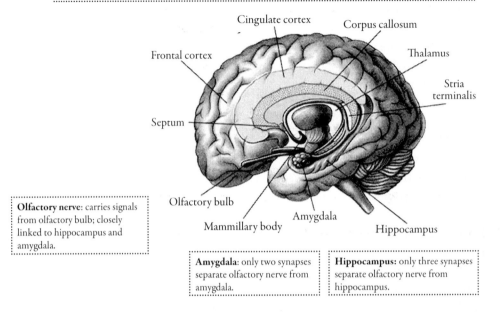

SMELL AND MEMORY
The olfactory bulb is in the limbic system, close to the amygdala (associated with emotion) and the hippocampus (associated with memory). When you first encounter a smell, it becomes linked to the emotions you associate with the events of that time. Encountering the smell again may trigger this link, evoking the memory and associated emotion.

Cingulate cortex

Corpus callosum

Frontal cortex

Thalamus

Stria terminalis

Septum

Olfactory nerve: carries signals from olfactory bulb; closely linked to hippocampus and amygdala.

Olfactory bulb

Amygdala

Mammillary body

Hippocampus

Amygdala: only two synapses separate olfactory nerve from amygdala.

Hippocampus: only three synapses separate olfactory nerve from hippocampus.

Figure 2.2. Smell and memory (image retrieved from www.buzzle.com/articles/amygdala-function.html).

Research shows that a memory of a visual image is likely to fade within days, but the memory of a smell may persist for up to a year or even decades (Carter *et al.*, 2014).

As a summary of this section, it can be stated that except mood, emotional states were affected by odours. In this way, a study carried out at the Rockefeller University showed that in the short term we remember just 1% of what we touch, 2% of what we hear, 5% of what we see, 15% of what we taste, and 35% of what we smell. The human olfactory system developed on a primal level to identify foods and sources, spoilage, and other dangers, but it did not stop here. The sense of smell is directly linked to the emotional, or limbic, system of the brain, which controls physiological and emotional responses, including pleasure, anger, and appetite. When we smell an aroma, our memory and emotions are jogged. Aromas, especially of food, can conjure up memories of long ago and, depending on whether the person had a positive or negative experience when smelling that aroma, the person will either be attracted or repelled by the scent, states Lempert (2002).

2.4 Odours and air quality

Too high or low temperatures or the lack of fresh air are the phenomena with which everyone met in some building. People spend more than 80% of their time inside of buildings; therefore, according to the publication of 'Indoor Air Quality Research', it is important to consider all aspects of the internal environment affecting the overall well-being, health and performance of the users in spaces (e.g. offices, production halls, shopping centres, etc.) (WHO, 2006). The space in buildings is made up of various environment components including inside air conditioning, humidity and atmospheric conditions (Földváry and Petraš, 2014). The internal or enclosures environment components can be divided into (Kapalo, 2009):

▸ physical (heat, humidity, light, sound, electric fields, static electricity, aero ions);
▸ chemicals (toxicants, aerosols, odorous substances);
▸ biological (microorganisms, bacteria, biological allergens (pollen, fur); and
▸ psychic (type of work, method of organization).

In the case of physical factors, their limited values as well as the process of measurement are described by national or international standards (Molina *et al.*, 1989). Quality assessment of the internal environment must, therefore, cover not only the lighting, vibration, thermal comfort, as well as indoor air quality too, which is affected by many factors, but also it must determine the concentration of various pollutants, ventilation rates, spatial distribution, chemical reactions of pollutants and air as a medium of communication used (TZB portal, 2016). The issue of indoor air quality in buildings and its impact on health, performance, and man feelings is getting increased attention since the late 70's of the 20th century. Providing an acceptable indoor air quality is associated with the analysis of the chemical composition of indoor air and solids. It should provide sufficient fresh air, reduce the concentration of pollutants to a level which does not adversely affect health and well-being of users under their limited values, and ensure the minimum presence of odour substances in the indoor environment. Excessive ventilation causes energy loss and, conversely, lack of ventilation causes unsatisfactory quality of indoor air. In this regard, a balance with adjustable regulation of the level and method of ventilation using heat and moisture conditioners and the control of the occurrence of pollutants in the environment should be ensured (Šenitková *et al.*, 1999; Vilčeková, 2009).

Quality of indoor environment is among the areas to be evaluated in all systems of a comprehensive environmental assessment of buildings. The main indicators of internal environment' evaluation in selected systems of environmental assessments of buildings is shown in Table 2.2.

Table 2.2. Indicators of building internal environment evaluation (data retrieved from Vilčeková, 2009).

System	Area of evaluation	Indicators of evaluation
CASBEE (Japan)	Internal environment	Noise and acoustics, heat comfort, brightness and lighting, air quality
BREEAM (UK)	Health and relax	Internal and external questions influencing health and relax (lighting, air quality, dangerous materials, radon, internal noise, system of heat water)
SBTool (28 world countries)	Quality of internal environment	Quality of internal air, ventilation, air temperature and relatively humidity, daily light and lighting, noise and acoustics, electromagnetic pollution
LEED (USA)	Quality of internal environment	Quality of internal environment, pollution control from smoking, monitoring of CO_2, increasing of ventilation, managerial plans IAQ, low emitting materials, control of harmful substances 'sources and chemicals, thermal comfort
Green Globes (Canada)	Internal environment	Effectiveness of ventilation system, control of sources or internal pollution, proposal of lighting and integration of illuminating system, thermal and acoustics comfort
HK-Beam (Hong Kong)	Quality of internal environment	Thermal comfort, ventilation, quality of internal air, natural lighting, artificial lighting, noise and vibration
NABERS (Australia)	Interior	The nature of the weapons site, equipment and service, percentage of job positions in far of 5 metres from the windows, percentage of workers able to control, lighting of work place

The requirements for internal air quality are controlled by American Standard ASHRAE 62 (Ventilation for acceptable indoor air quality) in USA and in some others countries (ANSI/ASHREA, 2001), while in many European countries, as well as in some others, it is regulated by European norm *prEN 13779* (CEN, prEn13779, 1999). These two documents are not the same and have some differences. American norm lays down the minimum value of 8 litres per second per person for required amount of fresh air in the spaces on base of internal maximum concentration of CO_2 of 700 ppm (mg/l). The European Standard defines three levels of performance: IDA1, IDA2, IDA3 based on a concentration of CO_2 in 800, 1000, and 1,500 ppm. It is likely that the strictest European requirement IDA1 is more moderate than the one requested by ASHRAE. In the spaces where smoking is forbidden, prEN 13779 allows the ventilation with a speed of 4 litres per second per person for a degree IDA3; it is a half air speed exchange as in the case of ASHRAE. There is also a local Israeli regulation, which is at the phase of preparation; its goal is to suggest the compromises between both previous documents (Javorček and Sternová, 2016). The essential requirements from the perspective of internal climate on that (what is pleasant), are provided by European standards:

▸ EN 15251 Indoor environmental input parameters for design and assessment of energy performance of buildings-addressing indoor air quality, thermal environment, lighting and acoustics;
▸ Directive 2010/31/EU of the European parliament and of the council of 19 May 2010 on the energy performance of buildings;
▸ ISO EN 7730 Moderate Thermal Environments;
▸ CR 1752 Ventilation for Buildings – Design Criteria for The Indoor Environment;
▸ EN 13779 Ventilation for non-residential buildings – Performance requirements for ventilation and room-conditioning systems;
▸ EN ISO 7726 Ergonomics of the thermal environment – Instruments for measuring physical quantities; and,
▸ EN 12599 Ventilation for buildings – Test procedures and measurement methods to hand over air conditioning and ventilation systems.

Standards and guidelines for estimating the required minimum ventilation rates are currently available and are far from complete. In this context, users mainly have two requirements:
▸ health risk of inhaled air should be negligible; and
▸ air should be felt fresh and pleasant.

According to the American society of engineers for heating, cooling, and air treatment (ASHRAE), the acceptable air quality can be defined as 'an air in which there are no known pollution in harmful concentrations determined by the competent authorities, with which the majority (80% or more) people exposed do not reflect dissatisfaction' (ANSI/ASHREA, 2001). People produce carbon dioxide (CO_2) in proportion to the level of their metabolism (Seppänen *et al.*, 1999). In terms of quantity, it is the most important pollution made by people. At low concentrations, the inner CO_2 is not harmful and, then, people do not feel it. CO_2 has been successfully used as indicator of pollution produced by humans for over a century (Hurtíková and Petráš, 2014). The main indicators from the perspective of air quality are (Šabíková, 2002):
▸ high, low or unstable temperature;
▸ concentration of CO_2 in an air;
▸ intensity of relative humidity;
▸ air velocity; and
▸ presence of smoke, odours, dust, dirt, and mildew too.

In terms of comfort, there are many residents which include the link between carbon dioxide and indoor air quality (Földváry and Petraš, 2014). If in a limited space, there is a high concentration of CO_2, it emerges a dissatisfaction and sleepy feeling, what ultimately discourage people from a long-term stay in this area. The fresh air contains about 400 mg/l of CO_2, and in a classic room, the concentration of CO_2 can be doubled in just 1 h. This applies when 1 person stays at a rest; if in a room there are more people, who moreover do some physical activity (e.g. shopping, moving), it is necessary to maintain the air quality by replacing the volume of air in the room several times per hour (Table 2.3). An equally important factor of quality indoor air is its temperature. So how could be a person be discouraged from purchasing or time spending because of low temperature? On the contrary, he/she may be demotivated because of too warm environment, which in combination with high concentrations of CO_2 represents the worst case scenario for a given place, because the indoor environment in any building is a result of the interaction between the site, climate, building system, construction techniques, contaminant sources and building occupants (Berčík *et al.*, 2016a).

Table 2.3. The classes of activities (based on Vilčeková, 2009).

Class	Total energy output q_m (W/ m²)	q_m (met)	Examples of activities
0	≤65	≤1.12	Peaceful lying, relaxed lying (rest, watching TV)
1a	66-80	1.13-1.38	Seating activity with minimum of moving activity (administration, students in a rooms, control activity), seating activity connected with light manual hand/ shoulder-work (PC job, laboratory work, selecting of mini products)
1b	81-105	1.39-1.81	Seating activity with manual hand/shoulder/feet-work (outlet control, driving a car), standing activity something connected with slow walking with light obstacles moving or with overcoming of resistance (cooking, machine treatment and assembly of small parts, piece work of mechanics, service staff, shopping)
1c	106-130	1.82-2.23	Seating activity with regular using of both hands/ shoulders/ feet's (work in food sector and in kitchens, machine treatment and assembly of hard parts, driving a truck, tractors), standing activity with permanent using of both hands/ shoulders/ feet's in moving of more than 10 kilos of materials (shop assistants by a big frequency of customers, painting, welding, managing of drilling-machine, of lathe and moving of light trolleys), slow walking on a flat

Table 2.3 shows that optimum climatic conditions in different areas are different according to the performance of individual activities. For example, the temperature in grocery stores is ranging from 19 to 24 °C, while it is finding of a compromise between the implementation of activities, pleasant environment in terms of consumer perceptions, as well as to all conditions of storage for display in various departments. Retails must use climatic units to achieve the required level of temperature and CO_2 concentration in the individual food department. In the foreground is another important factor, relative humidity. The air in the stores must not be too dry, but, on the other hand, not too moist. The optimal level is between 30-70% saturation of the air with water vapour (Berčík, 2015).

In Table 2.4, the optimal and acceptable conditions of heat and humidity for a warm micro-climate period in a year are illustrated.

According to Vietoris *et al.* (2017), in addition to ensuring the optimal air quality, it is necessary to pay attention in eliminating unwanted odours. A typical example can be departments of animal feed with a specific odour in food stores. The sense of space aromatization for the purpose of stimulating (positive emotions, higher labour productivity, reducing nervousness, etc.) acquires the desired effect and force only when it reached a certain standard of indoor air quality (normal air temperature, humidity, neutralization of undesirable odours and breathable air).

Table 2.4. Examples of optimal and acceptable conditions of heat-humidity micro clime for warm period in a year (based on Vilčeková, 2009).

Work Class	Operative temperature (°C)		Acceptable speed of air ventilation v_a (m/ s)	Acceptable relative air humidity (%)
	Optimal	Acceptable		
0	25-28	20-29	≤0.2	
1a	23-27	20-28	≤0.25	30-70
1b	22-25	19-27	≤0.3	
1c	20-24	17-26	≤0.3	

2.5 Deploying scent in the marketplace and aroma marketing

When asked to compare a pair of shoes in a scented store and in un-scented store, 84% of customers reported that they were more likely to buy from the scented boutique

(Alan R. Hirsch)

2.5.1 Historical background of aroma marketing

Already in Egypt, more than 5,000 years ago, they used the power of using flavourings to mask the smell of the burning blood of their victims. In Rome, in turn, they involved animals, such as doves, which spread fragrances into the rooms at various social events. But smell, as such, was also used on two-floor trains during the war time, to inject courage to the fighters. Greeks used ceramic vases for storing scented essences to be used in massaging their legendary athletes. In China, traders came to the smarter way to sell their silk and used different essential oils to attract customers, in a very clever way. One of the first studies drawing attention to the significance of scent within the marketing industry occurred in 1932. In this research, tests were conducted exploring the relationship between a products odour, and consumer's perceptions of its quality level. During this study, women were exposed to a number of nylon stockings; each pair had a faint narcissus, fruit, sachet, or natural scent (somewhat unpleasant) (Clark, 2009; Fitzgerald and Swati, 2008).

Later, in the 1969, links between scent and both sales and consumers' perceptions of product quality were again evaluated and identified. In this study, Cox (1969) reported, nylon stockings with an orange odour sold better than unscented stockings. Approximately 90% of the women selected the orange-scented over the unscented version. Many of the women felt that the scented stockings were of better quality than the unscented ones (Clark, 2009).

In the 1970's, fragrances also began to gain recognition as a tool for retailers. During this time, the study of aromatherapy also became more widely accepted. Indeed, aromatherapy, enhancing the smells of indoor environments by introducing specific aromas, first became fashionable in the late 70's (Schifferstein and Block, 2002). Also in the retail environment, the next widely documented study demonstrating the significance of scent as a marketing tool involved linking consumer perceptions of products with fragrance placed directly at the point of sale. In this situation, research was conducted analysing the influence of scent on consumers purchase intent. In turn, 'Scratch and Sniff Stickers' represented one of the next milestones for scent in the marketing industry, in the 1980's in North America (Smellstickers.com, 2008). In the 1970's marketers began to find that smell could be used in brand promotion. They were also able to adjust the scent of their products to make them more palatable for the consumer.

Olfactory Marketing started back in the 1980's when British supermarkets discovered that if they had a bakery in a supermarket, the smell of fresh baking bread helped them sell not just more bread, but more other products from supermarket' portfolio, what is also influenced by placing of bakery department in a store (Hanlon, 2005). In 1982, further recognition of the significance of scent in the marketing industry occurred, when the Olfactory Research Fund coined the term 'aromachology'. Of note for marketing, this area of expertise is concerned only with the temporary effects of fragrances on human behaviour, feelings, of well-being, moods, and emotions. (Clark, 2009; Olfactory Research Fund, 2008).

2.5.2 Scent in marketing

> You can close your eyes, cover your ears, refrain from touch, and reject taste, but smell is a part of the air we breathe
>
> (Lindström, 2010)

The shops which apply scents, give their customers the feeling that they spend less time viewing goods, and testing them (Bradford and Desrochers, 2009; Levy *et al.,* 2012). Fragrance has become an important factor for the trader, which can slow the flow of customers in the store. The compatibility with the environment plays an important role, when odour is placed in a closed store (Sikela, 2014). Fiore *et al.* (2000) wrote that scent had an effect on affective state that partly mediated the effect on attitudes towards products and approach behaviours. The aroma could be used in marketing in many parts, such as marketer scent, product scent, ambient scent (Figure 2.3). Research has shown that suitable application of aromas contributes to the following facts:
▸ customers better and deeper evaluate a store;
▸ customers better perceive a value of offered products and services; and
▸ customers have a subconscious tendency to return to the place, where the flavouring was applied (Scentair, 2015).

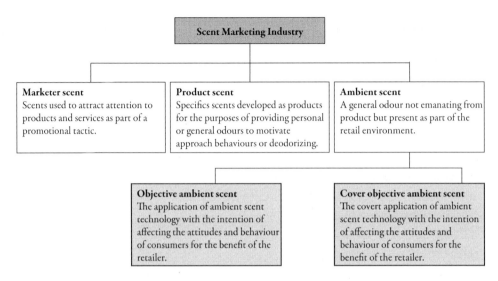

Figure 2.3. The use of scents to influence consumers (Bradford and Desrochers, 2009).

It is assumed that a scent is a sensory experience of smell perceived by a human being (Tarczydło, 2014). Scents are unique, just like fingerprints. For thousands of years, humans have used the power of scents for different purposes: (1) protection; (2) camouflage; (3) beauty; and (4) distinguishment (Emsenhuber, 2009; Vietoris, 2008). Figure 2.4 shows three types of odours: (1) head; (2) heart; and (3) basic (Saidl and Meravá, 2012; Štetka, 2012). Head notes are generally smaller, lighter molecules which dazzle and invigorate. They are usually fresh citrus or green notes, include lemon, lime, neroli, bergamot, grapefruit and fresher herbaceous notes like lavender, thyme and basil. Molecules of heart notes tend to be larger and smoother and can take anywhere from five minutes to an hour to develop. They can include different ingredients including flowers, spices, woods, resins and grasses. Finally, base notes have the largest, heaviest molecules. They are the notes that many clients are attracted to, such as woods, resins, oakmoss, vanilla, amber and musk. Smell is linked to pleasure and well-being, emotion, and memory. Therefore, it can influence customers' emotional state and mood to make the customers more susceptible to impact customer behaviour (Lindström, 2010).

Diffusing the right aroma can reinforce brand identity, create the perfect ambiance for clients, employees and guests, and differentiate our own business from competitors (Herz, 2009). Linked to changes in technologies for the production and distribution of scents, fragrance is used to shape consumer action, specifically attention, and purchase acts. The aroma use is a part of a recent recognition that branding needs to work through the emotions (with scent marketing itself, marketed through the promise that smell works directly on the

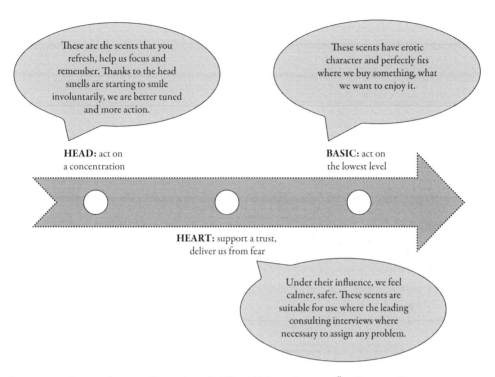

Figure 2.4. Types of scents (based on Saidl and Meravá, 2012; Štetka, 2012).

limbic system), but also forms part of a longer term emphasis on the active shaping of retail atmospherics, wrote Anderson (2014). Scent is used to create a pleasant ambient, create a signature for a brand, or convey a specific scent naturally associated with a product; in this way, scent can increase vividness of a stimulus through concreteness (Kardes *et al.*, 2014).

The benefits of using scents in marketing are, among others:
- scents can help boost sales: it can trigger instant emotional reactions from customers and scent marketing can, thus, be very effective in boosting sales;
- scents make customers linger: the subjects were more likely to look around and browse through products in the rooms that were scented, and reported more positive opinions and a tendency to wait longer in lines in the fake store than its unscented counterpart;
- scents help create brand image: they are helpful in making people remember you, or to create associations in their minds; this is why it can be useful it creating an all rounded brand image; and,
- scents create a perception of quality: customers tend to perceive a scented product or space as being of better quality and will be willing to pay more when shopping in a scented store (Cartwright, 2014).

2.5.3 Definition of aroma marketing

> Initially, customers thought, that they spent 45 minutes in a shop, while their real time was 40 minutes (store without smell). The perception was changed after odour placing; they thought, they spent only 25 minutes, while their real time was over 60 minutes
>
> (Galeries Lafayette, 2014)

Aroma, scent or olfactory marketing is more than just diffusing a pleasant fragrance in a space. It is the art of taking a company's brand identity, marketing messages, target audience and creating a scent that amplifies these values. Baron (1997) concluded that much higher levels of positive affect were reported when participants were exposed to pleasant ambient scent and a positive state (happiness) that can be created by means of odours (De Groot *et al.,* 2015). The expression 'scent marketing' has been used to describe using scent to set a mood, promote products or position a brand and, thus, scents marketing can be defined as the strategic use of scent and olfactory experience in relation to commercial products (Anderson, 2014; Vlahos, 2007). Aroma marketing as one of modern form of marketing increases the store image and brings to customers the new shopping experience (Sikela, 2014). Scent marketing has got two ways:

▶ ambient scenting, fill spaces in certain types of scents, such as the smell of coffee; and
▶ scent branding, creating a specific scent identifying mark (Scentmarketing, 2016).

Müller *et al.* (2011) differentiated between three forms of scent marketing, depending on how scents were used: (1) the marketer scent; (2) the product scent; and (3) the ambient scent. The Scent Marketing Institute estimates that number of odour will reach more than 500 million by 2016-2017. Professional aroma spaces (scent marketing) have a positive effect in all psychographic directions and are suitable for long-term increase in turnover (Stöhra, 1998). Aroma marketing is a series of incidents in which it is possible, with an impact of scents, to stimulate customers to buy goods and services and workers to be more active. It is scientifically proven that the information that is perceived by smell, affects directly and immediately the buying decision. Advertising agencies attribute to odour much more than just release a pleasant fragrance; in fact, it is a tool with a wide range of use (can stimulate, revitalize, create a feeling of relaxation, balance, peace, awakens memories, inspiration, feelings). Fragrances are used with the specific aim, to increase the profits and sales (Pajonk and Plevová, 2015). Scent marketing uses different diffusers or aroma techniques, while fragrances are adapted to profile a target consumer group (Jurášková *et al.,* 2012).

The importance of aroma marketing relies on several factors:
► the application of good air quality, it can consciously help to change or improve current mood, not only of customers but also of employees;
► scent marketing has a positive impact on customers, it makes them to become more generous;
► its placing allows to achieve increased sales; and,
► products and services are offered in a particularly favourable way.

Kardes *et al.* (2014) reported that scent marketing is a special branch of sensory marketing that studies and uses the enormous potential of perfume as a means of communication, emotion, and memory. Holliman (2011) describes aroma marketing as 'marketing without dollars'. Ambient scent is popularly believed to have the potential to create positive mood states, which will, then, translate into more favourable store and product evaluations and eventually into higher sales revenues (Krishna, 2010). It becomes 'permanent memory' (Levy *et al.,* 2012). According to Pabian (2011), aroma marketing signifies:
► exerting influence on the customer behaviour in the place of sales by using individually selected compositions of aromas;
► the art of using scents in the marketing campaign and accessing the customer's emotions;
► a significant element supporting modern marketing strategies and a part of the marketing mix;
► an exceptionally effective business tool; and,
► a powerful weapon in the fight for a customer, as one cannot resist the magic of scents, may close eyes and block the ears but we cannot stop breathing.

Kimmel (2012) gave some advices when using aroma marketing:
► test aromas on 'real' customers and get feedback before making final decision;
► do not overwhelm customers with a particular fragrance;
► make brand scent as specific and original as possible; so, there is a unique association with company brand;
► scent marketing works best with just a single aroma, so avoid complicated fragrances;
► think about the fact that what others smells might be nearby;
► brand fragrances can work best when there is already a particular association with a product and a particular smell in people's minds; and,
► do not let the scent expert to select the scent far away from the location where the product is being sold.

Scent marketing has different uses for different business, and so can be effectively divided into four distinct types (Cartwright, 2014):

- The aroma billboard smell, which makes the boldest scent statement; the customers are consciously aware of it, and the smell is part of the customer experience and is what consciously attracts attention.
- A thematic smell complements the décor or purpose of the place, such as vanilla or lavender smells at a beauty spa or a resort.
- Ambient smells are subtler and create an atmosphere, used to cover unpleasant odours or to fill a void.
- A signature smell is exclusive to a big brand name and is used to create a brand image; customers associate this smell with their favourite brand and what it represents.

2.6 Olfactory brand and product marketing

The brand is no longer just seen and heard, but also smelled

(Orange Slovakia)

There are several ways marketers can use the sense of smell to reach customers. The first, and perhaps most significant, is branding. Olfactory product marketing is a bit more straightforward but is still important. In that same environment, though, there may be many other aroma marketing techniques in use, either intentionally or not (Dooley, 2012). Scent can play an important role in differentiating brands in the market place, as well as improving consumer's satisfaction levels and sense of well-being in market place settings (Vlahos, 2007). The keys to olfactory branding are consistency and uniqueness. Aromatising and neutralising scents is performed not only to refresh the air but also to create a proper background for presentation of the company offer, to improve its perception, or to create a unique brand image. In fact, a brand specific odour is likely to evoke connections to the brand and strengthen the brand identity (Prarthana, 2014; Schmitt and Simonson, 1997). Spangenberg *et al.* (2006) found that shoppers spent more money in a clothing store, when the scent that was emitted in a particular department was congruent with the type of clothing being sold (i.e. a feminine/masculine scent emitted into the women's/men's department).

Morrin (2010) found that emitting a pleasant scent into shopping mall increased expenditures, but only among more contemplative shoppers or those who did not make unplanned purchase. The main target of scent marketing is the creation of a pleasant atmosphere for clients (Kardes *et al.*, 2014; Tarczydło, 2014). The use of piped-in aromas to set a mood, promote products or position a brand. Dave Van Epps, president of ScentAir (2015), a producer of aroma-marketing systems, told scent marketing, whether for condos or cars, is part of a broader movement known as full sensory branding, 'the key principle is that to be successful in an advertisement crammed world, companies must reach consumers not only through the overtaxed avenues of sight and sound but also through touch, taste and smell' (Vlahos, 2007).

Brand image is: (1) a set of opinions, judgements, and images held by stakeholders; (2) something like a symbolic brand superstructure; (3) tangible convictions allowing for enhancement of an individual's self-image; or finally (4) intangible factors/images significantly impacting the human behaviour in the market (Tarczydło, 2014). According to Lindström (2010), the smell is used in branding because it increases the customers' remembrance of the brand. It can create instant connections between a brand and other memories. Fragrances also contribute to raising awareness and brand recognition. There are cases where companies use a specific smell as a registered trademark. Companies seek in these cases the association of a specific odour with brands; it is a so-called 'signature fragrance' (Douce *et al.*, 2013; Hultén *et al.*, 2009; Jitpleecheep, 2011; Košťál', 2006).

Neuromarketing research has begun to focus on these sensory aspects (aroma, lighting, sounds, interior, and others visual elements) of shopping. Neuromarketing firms have arisen, and are specialised in testing sensory effects and advising retailers on sensory best practices. Smell is increasingly exploited by retailers using piped-in fragrances to trigger associations and activate goals related to a purchase (Genco, Pohlmann and Steidl, 2013). Scent marketing relies on the neuropsychological processing of olfactory stimuli in the human brain. The area of research which analyses neuropsychological effects of advertising and commercial activities on the consumer is called 'neuroeconomics' (Berčík *et al.*, 2016b). The term 'scent marketing' defines a subarea of the neuroeconomic research and describes the usage of scents for marketing purpose (Carter *et al.*, 2014; Dooley, 2012; Gulas and Bloch, 1995; Solomon, 2010).

2.6.1 Practical examples in product and service segment

> Let´s not forget that the little emotions are the great captains of our lives and
> we obey them without realizing it
>
> (Vincent Van Gogh)

Alankin (2016) published that the aroma marketing services may include:
▸ creation of a scent logo/corporate aroma;
▸ distributing bioactive fragrance compositions indoors (the method of scent space), considering the given industry specificity, and consequently special composition for: art galleries, travel agencies, fitness clubs, medical and dental practices, etc.;
▸ influencing the customer behaviour in the point of sale (scent post), reaching out to the customer's consciousness and sub-consciousness, creating emotions;

- atomising fragrance compositions related to the brand of the product during events, promotional activities, fairs (scent event), influencing the customer's sense of wellbeing, creating atmosphere and therefore facilitating friendly communication which is of vital importance in business relations; and,
- using scent in an advertising campaign (scent advertisement), e.g. in the form of products made by applying the scent print technology.

Sensory branding stimulates a consumer's relationship with a brand and cultivates an emotional connection by incorporating scent from a design perspective; this can empower an environment, and optimize brand loyalty. Below we provide a summary of brands or companies that apply aroma marketing in practice.

Citroën C4 perfume diffuser programme

- Citroen C4, offering as standard a scent-diffuser in the ventilation system and a range of nine different scents; customers may choose vanilla, lavender or citrus odour.
- A feature of the C4 is based on the fact that smells can have a significant effect on mood and sense of well-being, very pleasant environment for users of the C4; the perfumes also have ability to inspire an environment that is favourable to safe driving.
- Citroen test marketed the idea of perfume diffuser kit with a special edition Citroen C3 in 2003; the C3 Buddha Bar, which offered five difference fragrances based on the theme of Feng Shui (Hanlon, 2005; Hultén et al., 2009).

Nike shoes

- An experiment conducted, two identical pairs of Nike running shoes were placed in two separate, but identical, rooms; one room was infused with a mixed floral scent and the other was not. Test subjects inspected the shoes in each room and, then, answered a questionnaire.
- 85% customer's preferred the shoes displayed in the room with the fragrance and also estimated the value of the scented shoes on average to be $10.33 (9.48 €) higher than the pair of shoes in the unscented room (Aromaone, 2016b; Prarthana, 2014).

Digital flex media leader in CD and DVD

- Announced the launch of a line of Rub'n Smell discs. These discs help businesses, marketers and advertisers to cost-effectively connect and influence their target markets with scent marketing. The scent was incorporated into the ink and varnish was used to coat the company's disks.
- Scents such as fresh fruit, flowers, coffee, pizza, chocolate and custom scents and fragrances supplied by clients were used on the disks. The scent was activated when rubbed and lasted for a few seconds each time.

▸ These disks could retain their scent for years and the intensity of the smell could be controlled by scenting a larger or smaller area (Prarthana, 2014).

Bloom grocery stores: 'smell of grilling steak'

▸ Designed by ScentAir Ltd. in Mooresville, NC, USA.
▸ Billboard displays impaled piece of beef; inside this billboard a fan was installed that scatters to the surroundings the smell of black pepper and charcoal, which customers use when cooking the beef (Frucci, 2010).

McCain Corp.: 'baked potato-scented frozen aisles'

▸ Up to 500 Tesco and Asda stores are set to install scented displays that waft the aroma of jacket potatoes through the frozen aisles when a customer presses the front of the unit. It has created '3-D baked potatoes' that fill bus shelters across the U.K. with the smell of the baking potato.
▸ When people press a button on a poster, a hidden heating element warms the fiberglass 3-D potato and releases the aroma of oven-baked jacket potato throughout the bus shelter (Advertising Age, 2012; Magda, 2013).

New Balance shoe store

▸ In Beijing, a consulting firm introduced Chinese shoppers to the U.S. brand through a sensory store experience. A nostalgic wood and leather scent was used to convey the heritage and craftsmanship of the brand.
▸ Shoppers spent twice as much money as compared to similarly sized stores elsewhere; the atmosphere induced them to linger longer (Equal Strategy consulting firm, 2016).

California milk processor: 'Got Milk? Campaign'

▸ In a campaign intended to boost US sales of milk, the California board set up a device that emitted the fragrance of fresh-baked chocolate chip cookies from advertisements posted in San Francisco bus shelters.
▸ Thus, bus users complained that the scent was inappropriate and city officials ordered the ads to be removed (Kimmel, 2012).

LG chocolate phone

▸ The campaign used chocolate-scented point-of-purchase store displays, accomplished by embedding plastic, scent-infused strips into the displays and by adding a scented varnish into the information posters.
▸ Bowls of Hershey Kisses chocolates also were placed on the counter, next to the phone displays, although the chocolate scent was inconsistent with the mobile phone product category.

▶ It effectively associated aroma to its chocolate brand identity, and likely contributed to the successful launch of the product. The scent provided a strong link to the brand name, which accounted for much of the campaign's success (Kimmel, 2012).

Kraft Foods
▶ It sponsored a special holiday issue of People magazine.
▶ Five of its ads in the issue allowed readers to rub a spot to experience the smell of a product being advertised, such as Chips Ahoy and Philadelphia Cream Cheese (Solomon, 2010).

Coty: off-screen activity
▶ The international campaign of a cosmetics group 'Coty' was done in a popular chain of cinemas in the Czech Republic, Slovakia, and Hungary.
▶ Spots were projected on movie screens and were supported by non-standard off-screen activities relying on techniques aroma marketing. Coty spots were placed on 316 movie screen in 22 cities in three European countries.
▶ The campaign was aimed at promoting perfumes in foyer cinemas. This was parallel added by ads of Calvin Klein, Chloé, Davidoff, Guess, David Beckham and Katy Perry perfumes. The results of this promotion are not published by Coty. (Marketingové noviny, 2014).

Nivea: (1) 'Nivea- smell of summer.' and (2) 'Buy one get one free'
▶ Aromatization in the commercial was first used by NIVEA in Germany; before a film in a cinema, during the commercials depicting the seashore and resting people, the aroma of the sunscreen was sprayed around the hall, and the advertisement was completed with the inscription: 'Nivea- smell of Summer'.
▶ Recall of the ad increased by 515% over viewers who had seen the ad without the scent.
▶ Another scent practice was also conducted as the branded scent bags for NIVEA were available in almost 1.000 drug stores (Digital marketing glossary, 2015; Smartnose, 2016; Strategistmedia, 2015).

Sony: 'to smell what the actor smells at that point in the movie.'
▶ The company Sony joined the fragrance battle with using a scent combining an admixture of mandarin and vanilla.
▶ This flavour was chosen not by chance, but because the company is interested in attracting the female audience. This invention will allow olfactory content to be overlaid onto the content of video games (Powell, 2014; Strategistmedia, 2015).

Samsung

▶ It was conducting a test of its new signature fragrance in its Samsung experience concept store. German inventors have already patented a mobile phone with a smell chip which allows sending and receiving smell messages.

▶ People were staying in the scented room for about 11 minutes longer than usual (Strategistmedia, 2015).

Apple computers

▶ Buyers of Apple computers, iPhones and other products, know them too well, even the smell of a new device.

▶ This very specific smell is rumoured to come from inside the devices, but some have suggested that the packaging is responsible for it. However, the plastic iPhone has the same smell as the aluminium MacBook, so the scent is probably not added to the plastic.

▶ Apple has never owned up to these tactics, but an Apple Mac scent has been produced by the Air Aroma company, combining the smells of cardboard, ink and other ingredients (Bevers, 2013).

Lipton tea brand

▶ In the Czech Republic the Lipton company launched an 'aroma ad'. They installed 3D pyramids from fruits, which look like bags of Lipton on the bus stations in Anděl and Florenc (Prague).

▶ There, an intensive tea fragrance was sprayed at 5 minutes intervals (Media Guru, 2012).

Nature et Découvertes

▶ The store atmosphere plays a prominent role; most consumers are stimulated by smell.

▶ Before consumers enter the store, a cedar smell is distributed. Consumers are first attracted by this scent, and then by the product range.

▶ Cedar scent was chosen because the smell of wood is closely connected with nature and represents a brand identity (Krofiánová, 2008).

Rolls-Royce

▶ In England, buyers began complaining in the mid-1990 that the new models just did not lie up to their earlier models. The company went to work to track down the problem.

▶ Rolls Royce reproduced the scent of his big seller, the 1965 Silver Cloud, and sprays it under the seats to recreate the scent of this classic 'Roller'. Rolls Royce has been known to use scent in their showrooms, alongside their beautiful cars.

▶ They reconstructed the classic scent, and now spray it under the seats of new vehicles (Brumfield, 2008).

Cadillac

▶ In USA the new-car smell, the real scent of factory freshness, is no longer just a project. General Motors recently revealed that its Cadillac division had engineered a scent for its vehicles and has been adding it into the leather seats.

▶ The scent was created in a laboratory, was picked by focus groups, and is now the aroma of every new Cadillac put on the road (Hakim, 2003).

Dunkin' Donuts: 'scent of coffee on Seoul buses'

▶ The company Dunkin' Donuts launched a campaign in South Korea, known as Flavour Radio. Air fresheners were installed on commuter buses in Seoul to lure in customers to their stores.

▶ These machines would release the aroma of Dunkin' Donuts coffee into the air as the sound of the company's advertisement was simultaneously played on the buses speakers. When the radio advertisement ended, the bus conveniently stopped close to a Dunkin' Donuts store.

▶ Coffee shops in Seoul increased by 16% their sales and especially the sales of Dunkin Donuts by the bus stops in Seoul increased by 29% (Aromaone, 2016a; Pastier, 2012; Tam, 2012).

Omni hotels: 'scratch-and-sniff tags'

▶ In 2006, the company Omni was pioneer in offering sensory branding as part of their public space amenities with the use of a green tea and lemongrass-infused scent in their lobbies and cappuccino-and mochaccino infused scenting in their coffees.

▶ The guests at Omni hotels received the papers with the patches smelling of blueberry muffins to encourage muffin purchases at the Starbucks located in the hotel lobbies (Ambius, 2016; Krishna, 2010).

Disney Corporation 'smellitzer'

▶ 'Smellitzer' is a device that shoots out carefully engineered scents the way a howitzer sprays bullets, a method for sequentially directing at least two different scents from a gaseous scent-emitting system, according to a US patent issued in 1986.

▶ Haunted Mansion is suitably dank and musty, and that the Pirates of the Caribbean ride evokes the smell of the sea (Keenan, 2014).

British Airways: 'making flying special'

▶ In fact, since 1999, British Airways (BA) has been scenting its business class lounge at Heathrow Airport with the smell of freshly cut grass and the ocean.

▶ BA was also a sponsor of the Fragrance Foundation's 2011 Jasmine Awards. It was only natural for them to take the leap into in cabin scent marketing (O'Keefe, 2013).

Singapore Airlines

▸ This company uses a scent called Stefan Floridian Waters to perfume the cabins of its airplanes.

▸ SA towels and lounges are perfumed with the scent of flowers (Bevers, 2013; Gains, 2013; Klara, 2012).

Orange Slovakia

▸ In 2012 in the shopping mall Aupark used specific aroma to increase shopping experience and connect brand with odour (Strategie, 2012).

KFC

▸ Research was done on the influence of aroma on guests. KFC got a good kick out of a spike in sales after they have invaded people's homes with the irresistible scent of their unique, one-of-a-kind spices and pulled them into their restaurants to pay them money for the real thing.

▸ 46.3% felt exciting, 31.3% were happy, 12.7% felt nothing, 9.0% were relaxed.

▸ KFC is piloting an 'scent-focused' campaign that delivered food filled mail to corporate mail rooms at the lunch time mail drop. The mail was contain chicken, a side item, and a biscuit aimed to release the aroma of fried chicken throughout the office and trigger the cravings of busy cubicle dwellers (Latasha et al., 2016).

The placing of pleasant fragrances, e.g. lavender, affects positively the mood of respondents performing stressful job, even if their performance was secondarily compared with respondents in non-aroma environment or environment with the scent of e.g. cloves (Ludvigson and Rottman, 1989). Respondents working in an environment with a pleasant aroma reported higher self-efficacy, to have higher goals and more likely to apply effective business strategies as people working in conditions without odour placing (Baron, 1990, 1997; Dalton, 1996, 2000; Dalton *et al.,* 2002). Berčík *et al.* (2016a), conducted research on how aroma compounds influenced the profit of a chosen pub-restaurant Sportpub Brezno and how influenced the sales of Panini's (baked baguettes) on base of implementation of aroma equipment (aroma dispenser). In the primary research, the researchers monitored daily sale (amount) of baked baguettes without using of aroma stimulus and, then, two kinds of fragrances were placed inside the pub restaurant. Both aroma fillings are mostly made from natural ingredients and they are produced under strictly view of IFRA (International Fragrance Association, www.ifraorg.org). An aroma of 'crunchy bread' was used in first two weeks, and after this, the last two weeks, a fragrance of 'chicken soup' was tested. The aroma compounds were placed in the middle of the pub restaurant Sportpub Brezno. After a total comparison of studied period (first month without aromatization and second month with aromatization) it was possible to state, that during the period in which aroma compounds were used the sales increased a 2.6% (on April, 2016). A possible explanation for the positive but minimal effects was that only one diffuser (aromatic compound designed for space with an area of 30 m²) was used in a pub restaurant of 120 m². There are more modern spraying methods based on the principle of nebulization (aroma particles 1000 times smaller in comparison to conventional aerosol freshener). Besides, during the research time at the Sportpub Brezno, the quality of the air (e.g. the amount of CO_2 particles, temperature, and humidity) was not constant.

2.7 Conclusions

Nowadays, customers can buy almost everything in the shops as well as online with a few simple clicks, but some companies are scrambling for ideas to bring consumer spending back to the physical realm. While TV, radio, the internet and print media appeal to consumer' senses of sight and sound, the sense of smell offers unique challenges to companies trying to attract attention. An era where the actual customer experience of being in a hotel, restaurant or retail store is becoming more and more important, then aroma marketing' research could be focused on placing the right fragrances on the right places. More modern stores are designed to maximise the impact of scent and create a multisensory experience. Many businesses are simply using 'real smells' in their advantage (except them, which are located in the big shopping malls, because they cannot change the central air conditions of mall) vs places, where the owners can and would like to influence the customers' smell sense. The future of this type of research is to conduct experiments in real, as well as in laboratory conditions. One of the most important survey goals of scent marketing for future are the odour impact on business profits, time spending by shopping, association between brands and gender, age, etc. Smell is one of most powerful senses which background in the industry taught customers the value of aroma. Researchers on the topic undoubtedly see the need to combine traditional approaches with consumer neuroscience (especially EEG, fMRI, FaceReader equipment). The use of this state-of-the-art techniques will help in finding explanations to questions such as how can aroma influence consumer decision in various business segments (for example: health service, production, administration, business, financial institutions, personal transportation, etc.)?

References

Advertising Age, 2012. Smell marketing: McCain's baked potato bus shelters. Available at: http://tinyurl.com/jrxrnhc.

Alankin, A., 2016. Multisensory experiential marketing. Experiential Marketing Blog. Eventige Media Group. Available at: http://tinyurl.com/mewuulq.

Ambius, 2016. The smell of success. Available at: http://tinyurl.com/lu8uucc.

Anderson, B., 2014. Encountering affect: capacities, apparatuses, conditions. Ashgate Publishing, New York, NY, USA, 202 pp.

ANSI/ASHREA Standard 62, 2001. Ventilation for acceptable indoor air quality. EN 14449. Guideline for ventilation requirements in buildings. American Society of Heating, Refrigerating and Air-Conditioning Engineers, Atlanta, GA, USA.

Araneda, R.C., Kini, A.D. and Firestein, S., 2000. The molecular receptive range of an odorant receptor. Nature Neuroscience 3: 1248-1255.

Aromaone, 2016a. Dunkin' donuts. Available at: http://www.aromaone.sk/dunkin-donuts.

Aromaone, 2016b. Nike. Available at: http://www.aromaone.sk/nike.

Barnea, G., O'Donnell, S., Mancia, F., Sun, X., Nemes, A., Mendelsohn, M. and Axel, R., 2004. Odorant receptors on axon termini in the brain. Science 304: 1468.

Baron, R.A., 1990. Environmentally induced positive affect: its impact on self-efficacy, task performance, negotiation, and conflict. Journal of Applied Social Psychology 20: 368-384.

Baron, R.A., 1997. The sweet smell of helping: effects of pleasant ambient fragrance on prosocial behaviour in shopping malls. Personality and Social Psychology Bulletin 23(5): 498-503.

Bensafi, M., Rouby, C., Farget, V., Bertrand, B., Vigouroux, M. and Holley, A., 2002. Influence of affective and cognitive judgments on autonomic parameters during inhalation of pleasant and unpleasant odors in humans. Neuroscience Letters 319(3): 162-166.

Berčík, J., 2015. Využitie neuromarketingu vo vizuálnom merchandising potravín (Using of neuromarketing in food visual merchandising). PhD-thesis, SUA, Nitra, Slovakia, 216 pp.

Berčík, J., Paluchová, J. and Horská, E., 2016. Neuroeconomics: an innovative view on consumer´s decision process. Journal of Business Management and Economics 4(8): 22-28.

Berčík, J., Paluchová, J., Vietoris, V. and Horská, E., 2016. Placing of aroma compounds by food sales promotion in chosen service business. Potravinárstvo Journal 10(1).

Bevers, S., 2013. 10 Weird sensory marketing tricks companies use on us. Available at: http://tinyurl.com/k58w6qe.

Bradford, K.D. and Desrochers, D.M., 2009. The use of scents to influence consumers: the sense of using scents to make cents. Journal of Business Ethics 90(2): 141-153.

Brumfield, C.R., 2008. Whiff! The revolution of scent communications in the information age. Quimby Press, New York, NY, USA.

Carter, R., Aldridge, S., Page, M. and Parker, S., 2014. The human brain book. DK Publishing, New York, NY, USA, 264 pp.

Cartwright, S., 2014. How and why businesses make use of scent marketing to boost sales. Available at: http://tinyurl.com/kbzwc8a.

CEN, European Committee for Standardization, 1999. prEn13779: E. Ventilation for buildings performance requirements for ventilation and air-conditioning systems. CEN, Brussels, Belgium.

Clark, P., 2009. Running head: management overview of Scent as a marketing communications tool. SMC Working Paper 3: 7.

Cox, D.F., 1969. The sorting rule model of the consumer product evaluation process. Risk taking and information handling in consumer behaviour. Graduate School of Business Administration, Harvard University, Boston, MA, USA, pp. 324-369.

Dalton, P., 1996. Odor perception and beliefs about risk. Chemical Senses 21(4):447-458.

Dalton, P., 2000. Fragrance perception: from the nose to the brain. Journal of Cosmetics Science 51: 141-151.

Dalton, P., Doolittle, N. and Breslin, P.A., 2002. Gender-specific induction of enhanced sensitivity to odors. Nature Neuroscience 5: 199-200.

De Groot, J.H.B., Smeets, M.A.M., Rowson, M.J., Bulshing, P.J., Blonk, C.G., Wilkinson, J.E. and Semin, G.R., 2015. A sniff of happiness. Psychological Science 1(17): 684-700.

Digital Marketing Glossary, 2015. What is scent marketing definition? Available at: http://tinyurl.com/mshlf62.

Dooley, R., 2012. Brainfluence. 100 Ways to persuade and convince consumers with neuromarketing. John Willey and Sons Inc., Hoboken, NJ, USA, 286 pp.

Doty, R.L., Applebaum, S., Zusho, H. and Settle, R.G., 1985. Sex differences in odor identification ability: a cross-cultural analysis. Neuropsychologia 23: 667-672.

Douce, L., Poels, K., Janssensa, W. and De Backerb, C., 2013. Smelling the books: the effect of chocolate scent on purchase-related behavior in a bookstore. Journal of Environmental Psychology 36: 65-69.

Emsenhuber, B., 2009. Scent marketing: subliminal advertising messages. Conjunction with informatik, Lübeck, Germany. Available at: http://tinyurl.com/mkasl9y.

Equal Strategy Consulting Firm, 2016. Available at: http://equalstrategy.com.

Fiore, A.M., Yah, X. and Yoh, E., 2000. Effects of a product display and environmental fragrancing on approach responses and pleasurable experiences. Psychology and Marketing 17: 27-54.

Fitzerald, P.B. and Swati, J., 2008. Olfaction as a cue for product quality. Kluwer Academic Publishers, Dordrecht, the Netherlands, 295 pp.

Földváry, V. and Petráš, D., 2014. Zabezpečenie kvality vzduchu a vetracie štandardy v bytových domoch (Ensuring of air quality and ventilation standards in residential buildings). Eurostav 20(9). Available at: http://tinyurl.com/m7gow82.

Frucci, A., 2010. The steak-scented billboard: advertising´s stinking future. Available at: http://tinyurl.com/mxwf3y6.

Gains, N., 2013. Brand essense: using sense, symbol and story to design brand identity. Kogan Page Publishers, Philadelphia, PA, USA, 232 pp.

Genco, S.J., Pohlmann, A.P. and Steidl, P., 2013. Neuromarketing for dummies. John Wiley and Sons Canada, Ltd., Mississauga, Canada, 392 pp.

Gulas, Ch. and Bloch, P., 1995, Right under our noses: ambient scent and consumer responses. Journal of Business and Psychology 10(1): 87-98.

Hakim, D., 2003. New luxury car specifications: Styling. Performance. Aroma. The New York Times. Available at: http://tinyurl.com/kqw2vo8.

Hanlon, M., 2005. Citroen adds a sense of smell to the new C4. Available at: http://newatlas.com/go/3643.

Havlicek, J. and Roberts, S.C., 2009. MHC-correlated mate choice in humans: a review. Psychoneuroendocrinology 34: 497-512.

Herz, R.S. and Inzlicht, M., 2002. Sex differences in response to physical and social factors involved in human mate selection: the importance of smell for women. Evolution and Human Behavior 23: 359-364.

Herz, R.S., 2009. Aromatherapy facts and fictions: a scientific analysis of olfactory effects on mood, physiology and behavior. International Journal of Neuroscience 119(2): 263-290.

Holliman, G., 2011. Marketing without dollars: successful marketing is more a MINDSET than a skill-set. Xlibris Corporation, Bloomington, IN, USA, 186 pp.

Hultén, B., Broweus, N. and Van Dijk, M., 2009. Sensory marketing. Springer, London, UK, 183 pp.

Hurtíková, D. and Petráš, D., 2014. The energy performance certificate of ventilation and evaluation of indoor air quality in office building in Slovakia. Indoor Air 2014. Proceedings of the 13th International Conference on Indoor Air Quality and Climate, Pokfulam, University of Hong Kong, Japan, pp. 650-656.

Imamura, K., Mataga, N. and Mori, K., 1992. Coding of odor molecules by mitral/ Tufted cells in rabbit olfactory bulb: I. aliphatic compounds. Journal of Neurophysiology 68: 1986-2002.

Iwema, C.L., Fang, H., Kurtz, D.B., Youngentob, S.L. and Schwob, J.E., 2004. Odorant receptor expression patterns are restored in lesion-recovered rat olfactory epithelium. Journal of Neuroscience 24: 356-369.

Javorček, M. and Sternová, Z., 2016. Hygienické parametre vnútorného prostredia v triede (Hygienic parametres of internal environment in a class). Správa budov. Available at: http://tinyurl.com/ka77s52.

Jitpleecheep, P., 2011. Sweet smell of opportunity. Available at: http://tinyurl.com/k54mjer.

Jurášková, O. and Horňák, P., 2012. Velký slovník marketingových komunikací (Bif dictionary of marketing communication). Grada Publishing, Prague, Czech Republic, 272 pp.

Kalat, J.W., 2014. Biological psychology. Cengage Learning EMEA, Hampshire, UK, 584 pp.

Kapalo, P., 2009. Legislatívne požiadavky na výmenu vzduchu v budovách (Legislative requirements for air exchange in the buildings). Plynár. Vodár. Kúrenár + Klimatizácia 7(5): 46-47.

Kardes, F.R., Cronley, M.L. and Cline, T.W., 2014. Consumer behaviour, 2nd edition. South-Western College Pub, Cincinnati, OH, USA, 576 pp.

Keenan, T.P., 2014. Technocreep: the surrender of privacy and the capitalization of intimacy. Friesens, Canada, 64 pp.

Kimmel, A., 2012. Psychological foundations of marketing. Routledge, New York, NY, USA, 282 pp.

Klara, R., 2012. Something in the air. In a growing trend, retailers are perfuming stores with near-subliminal scents. Call it branding's final frontier. Available at: http://tinyurl.com/lr6wp7p.

Knasko, S.C., Gilbert, A.N. and Sabini, J., 1990. Emotional state, physical well-being, and performance in the presence of feigned ambient odor. Journal of Applied Social Psychology 20(16): 1345-1357.

Košťál, D., 2006. Ponúknite viac zážitkov (Offer more experiences). Obchod Journal 11(5): 18-19.

Krishna, A., 2010. Sensory marketing: research on the sensuality of products. Taylor and Francis Group, Abingdon, UK, 396 pp.

Krofiánová, D., 2008. Jak působit na všech pět smyslu zákazníka? (How influence on all senses of customer?). Moderní obchod Journal: 62.

Latasha, K. *et al.*, 2016. Analyzing the impact of sensory marketing on consumers: A case study of KFC. Proceedings of the International Conference on Tourism, Hospitality and Marketing. 2016. Mauritius, University Mascarene Available at: http://tinyurl.com/m64mbex.

Lempert, P., 2002. Being the shopper: understanding the buyer′s choice. John Wiley and Sons, Hoboken, NJ, USA, 245 pp.

Levy, M., Weitz, A.B. and Grewal, D., 2012. Retail management. McGraw-Hill, New York, NY, USA, 675 pp.

Lin, D.Y., Shea, S.D. and Katz, L.C., 2006. Representation of natural stimuli in the rodent main olfactory bulb. Neuron 50: 937-949.

Lindström, M., 2010. Buyology: truth and lies about why we buy. Crown Business, UK, 272 pp.

Lorig, T.S., 2000. The application of electroencephalographic techniques to the study of human olfaction: a review and tutorial. International Journal of Psychophysiology 36(2): 91-104.

Ludvigson, H.W. and Rottman, T.R., 1989. Effects of ambient odors of lavender and cloves on cognition, memory, affect and mood. Chemical Senses 14(4): 525-536.

Magda, I., 2013. McCain marketing drive includes baked potato-scented frozen aisles. Available at: http://tinyurl.com/k4lajx5.

Marketingové noviny, 2014. Zahájena mezinárodní kampaň COTY, která využívá aroma-marketingu (International campaign Coty launched, uses aroma marketing). Available at: http://tinyurl.com/kql7s8y.

McGlone, F., Österbauer, R.A., Demattè, L.M. and Spence, Ch., 2013. The crossmodal influence of odor hedonics on facial attractiveness: behavioural and fMRI measures. In: Signorelli, F. and Chirchiglia, D. (eds.) Functional brain mapping and the endeavor to understand the working brain. InTech, Rijeka, Croatia, 522 pp.

MediaGuru. 2012. Lipton podporuje čaje netradičními zastávkami. Available at: http://tinyurl.com/mcneb7m.

Molina, C., Pickering, C.A.A. and De Bortoli, M., 1989. Indoor air quality and its impact on man, Sick building syndrome: a practical guide. EUR 12294 EN, Brussels, Belgium.

Morrin, M., 2010. Sensory marketing: research on the sensuality of products. Aradhna Krishna, New York, NY, USA, 80 pp.

Müller, J., Alt, F. and Michelis, D., 2011. Pervasive advertising human-computer interaction series. Springer Science and Business Media, London, UK, 366 pp.

Nef, P., 1998. How we smell: the molecular and cellular bases of olfaction. Psychological Sciences 13: 1-5.

Neumannn, P., 2011. Navoďte v predajni pocit pohody (Make a feeling of relax in a store). Tovar and Predaj Journal 1(1): 20-21.

O′Keefe, A., 2013. Scent marketing at British Airways. Available at: http://tinyurl.com/l8900wp.

Olfactory Research Fund, 2008. Aging well with your sense of smell: a handbook for baby boomers. Olfactory Research Fund, New York, NY, USA.

Pabian, A., 2011. Sensory marketing. Marketing i Rynek 1: 2-6.

Pajonk, P. and Plevová, K., 2015. Vnemový marketing – zmysly v podpore predaja (Sensory marketing – senses in sale promotion). Studia Commercialia Bratislavensia 87(29): 86-87.

Pastier, M., 2012. Rozhlasová reklama, ktorá aktivuje vôňu (Radio advertising, which activates an odour). Available at: http://tinyurl.com/m49lrza.

Pinto, R.J.C., Isabel, P.P.P., Xavier, M., Maria do Rosário A.C., Sílvio, J.P.S.M., 2014. Analysis of the human reaction to odors using electroencephalography responses. World Congress on Engineering. Available at: http://tinyurl.com/lcff8go.

Powell, M., 2014. The power of smell: scent marketing meets the future of gaming and internet surfing. Available at: http://tinyurl.com/l6544w7.

Pradeep, A.K., 2010. The buying brain. Secrets for selling to the subconscious mind. John Wiley and Sons, Inc., Hoboken, NJ, USA, 252 pp.

Prarthana, K., 2014. Multisensory marketing: creating sustainability perspective in various sectors. Asia-Pacific Journal of Management Research and Innovation 10(1): 89-95.

Rennaker, R.L., Chen, C.F.F., Ruyle, A.M., Sloan, A.M. and Wilson, D.A., 2007. Spatial and temporal distribution of odorant-evoked activity in the piriform cortex. Journal of Neuroscience 27: 1534-1542.

Šabíková, J., 2002. Indoor environment and health. Životné Prostredie Journalb 36(3). Available at: http://tinyurl.com/m6gezjg.

Saidl, J. and Meravá, T., 2012. Vůně pre intelektuály? A proč ne (Aroma for intelectuals? Why not). Trend Marketing 8(5): 32-33.

Scent marketing, 2016. Available at: http://www.scentmarketing.cz.

Scentair, 2015. Available at: http://www.scentair.com.

Schifferstein, H.N.J. and Block, S., 2002. The signal function of thematically. Congruent ambient scents in a retail environment. Oxford University Press, Oxford, UK.

Schmitt, B. and Simonson, A., 1997. Marketing aesthetics. Smartnose 2016. NIVEA scent bag. Free Press, New York, NY, USA. Available at: http://tinyurl.com/l7fm5qf.

Šenitková, I., Jesenská, Z., Piecková, E., Sternová, Z. and Števulová, N., 1999. Škodliviny negatívne pôsobiace na zdravie. Budovy na bývanie (Pollutants that negatively affect health. Residential buildings). Ministerstvo výstavby a verejných prác SR, Bratislava, Slovakia, 187 pp.

Seppänen, O.A., Fisk, W.J. and Mendell, M.J., 1999. Association of ventilation rates and CO_2 concentrations with health and other responds in commercial and industrial buildings. Indoor Air 9: 226-252.

Sikela, H., 2014. Čuch je významný zmysel (Smell is an important sense). Slovenský výber Journal 2(18): 26.

Smartnose, 2016. Scratch and sniff. Available at: http://www.smartnose.net.

Smellstickers, 2016. Available at: http://www.smellstickers.com.

Solomon, M.R., 2010. Sensory marketing: Smells like profits. FT Press, Upper Saddle River, NJ, USA, 9 pp.

Spangenberg, E.R., Sprott, D.E., Grohmann, B. and Tracy, D.L., 2006. Gender-congruent ambient scent influences on approach and avoidance behaviors in a retail store. Journal of Business Research 59: 1281-1287.

Štetka, P., 2012. Scent marketing alebo aromamarketing. Útok predajcov na ďalší náš zmysel (Scent marketing or aroma marketing. Attack of sellers to further our sense). Available at: http://tinyurl.com/lmg6nnx.

Stöhra, A., 1998. Psychografická štúdia aromatozovaných priestorov. Available at: www.aromaone.sk/12578.

Strategie, 2012. Orange testate aroma marketing (Orange testes aroma marketing). Available at: http://tinyurl.com/lcrvd6y.

Strategistmedia, 2015. Getting into consumer´s mind with scent marketing. Available at: http://tinyurl.com/mu3s4yn.

Strotmann, J., Levai, O., Fleischer, J., Schwarzenbacher, K. and Breer, H., 2004. Olfactory receptors proteins in axonal processes of chemosensory neurons. Journal of Neuroscience 224: 7754-7761.

Tam, B., 2012. Scent of coffee on Seoul buses: what´s the marketing secret? Available at: http://www.cnbc.com/id/48676703.

Tarczydło, B., 2014. Scents and elements of aroma marketing in building of an appropriate brand image. Knowledge economy society – Managing organizations. Concepts and their applications. Cracow University of Economics, Cracow, Poland, 378 pp.

TZB Portal, 2016. Kvalita vzduchu v budovách (Air quality in the buildings). Available at: http://www.tzbportal.sk.

Uchida, N., Takahashi, Y.K., Tanifuji, M. and Mori, K., 2000. Odor maps in the mammalian olfactory bulb: domain organization and odorant structural features. Nature Neuroscience 3: 1035-1043.

Vietoris, V., 2008. Sensory analysis of food. SUA, Nitra, Slovakia, 75 pp.

Vilčeková, S., 2009. Environmentálne hodnotenie prostredia v budovách (Environmental evaluation of environment in the buildings). TZB Haustechnik. Available at: http://tinyurl.com/lh2oog7.

Vlahos, J., 2007. Scent and sensibility. The New York Times, USA. Available at: http://tinyurl.com/l6z8npa.

Warrenburg, S., 2005. Effects of fragrance on emotions: moods and physiology. Chemical Senses 30: 248-249.

World Health Organisation (WHO), 2006. Air quality guidelines. Global update 2005. Available at: http://tinyurl.com/nqhenbc.

Yousem, D.M., Maldjian, J.A., Siddiqi, F., Hummel, T., Alsop, D.C., Geckle, R.J., Bilker, W.B. and Doty, R.L., 1999. Gender effects on odor-stimulated functional magnetic resonance imaging: Brain Research 818: 480-487.

Zhang, X. and Firestein, S., 2002. The olfactory receptor gene superfamily of the mouse. Nature Neurosience 5: 124-133.

3. The sense of sight

M. Brugarolas and *L. Martínez-Carrasco*

Universidad Miguel Hernández de Elche, Escuela Politécnica Superior de Orihuela, Agroenvironmental Economics Department, Ctra. Beniel, km 3.2, 03312 Orihuela, Alicante, Spain; mbrugaro@umh.es

Abstract

In this chapter, the sense of sight and its importance in sensory marketing is widely discussed. The authors provide a comprehensive state of the art about the different product attributes perceived by sight, such as colour, shape, size or general appearance. They also provide a wide range of examples of how companies use marketing visual attributes to target consumers and get their products to be better identified and assessed. Another important contribution of this chapter is the discussion of how sensory marketing and the sense of sight can be used to address three of the major society current challenges: (1) the health of consumers; (2) food waste; and (3) conservation of biodiversity.

Keywords: visual attributes, colour, shape, size, marketing

3.1 Introduction

A new perspective of the sense of sight in marketing: addressing the current challenges of the food system

The sense of sight has been almost unanimously highlighted as the most relevant sense from the perception's point of view (Hekkert and Schifferstein, 2008; Hulten *et al.*, 2009; Krishna, 2012; Spence, 2002). Marketing research has dealt extensively with the sense of sight and its important role on the perception process. This is the reason why Krishna (2012), one of the leading specialists in sensory marketing, barely addressed sight in its latest review on the subject for considering it too explored.

Therefore, it seems difficult to make a new contribution about the sense of sight and sensory marketing. However, we believe that there are some issues that have been omitted in previous reviews and have a significant relevance, not only from a managerial point of view, but also with regards to the future of our society as a whole.

The superior value given to 'appearance', which often hides the inner reality, is an inherent characteristic of our current society. There is no doubt that the appearance is important, and for food this is also a fact: consumers wish to buy products that address their standards or aesthetic tastes, and to do so in places that they consider visually attractive. The failure to consider this premise decreases the value of the products and can even lead to market failure. This circumstance affects the whole value chain. Thus, preferences in colour, shape, and size of products can lead primary producers to grow only certain crop varieties or breeders to select species or cultivars based only on aesthetic criteria. This phenomenon might be one of the explanations of the loss of biodiversity that affects the world's agricultural ecosystems (Martínez-Carrasco *et al.*, 2015).

On the other hand, the exclusive consideration of aesthetic criteria when deciding whether to include or not a product in the food chain, also contributes to increase food waste, which currently affects between 30 and 50% of safe edible food (EC, 2014; Gustavsson *et al.* 2011). Both problems, loss of biodiversity and food waste are two of the food system's great challenges today.

Another issue regarding the relationship between external appearance of food and society challenges is related to diet and health. Indeed, low appealing foods, such as some vegetables or legumes, could be voluntarily reduced or excluded from consumer diets, regardless the effect that such exclusion may have on their health. In fact, the relationship between diet and certain non-communicable diseases (NCD) is a proven fact, and the incidence of these diseases is growing (Pérez-Farinós *et al.*, 2015). In addition, it must be remembered that health and well-being are key topics directly linked to labour force participation, productivity, and sustainability (Eurofound, 2013). Proof of the importance of the problem is that the WHO (World Health Organization) (2013) has developed a 'Global Action Plan on NCDs 2013-2020' to reduce its impact on the population.

Finally, it is worth to note that, in addition to these general problems affecting the whole society, the survival of companies and their competitiveness in the market is directly related to achieving consumer satisfaction and offering a product that is attractive to them. In this scenario, the adequate management and control of marketing variables, many of which are perceived by the sense of sight, is essential.

There are many features of a product that can be perceived by the sense of sight, either intrinsic or extrinsic, however consumer judgments take them as a whole. In this chapter, the authors will discuss how companies use marketing tools to target consumers and get their products to be better identified and assessed. In addition, the possibility of using this knowledge to improve our society, and, thus, to have a more sustainable future from a social, economic, and environmental point of view, in line with the latest trends in marketing (Kotler *et al.*, 2010) will be explained.

The chapter will be structured as follows. Initially, the importance of the sense of sight in sensory marketing will be defined, and later, the authors will focus on the product attributes perceived by sight, such as colour, shape, size or general appearance. Many of these attributes are widely used as marketing tools not directly related to the product, but to the promotion or display at the sale point, and will be considered as well. All over the text, specific examples where companies and organizations use sensory marketing tools directly related to the sense of sight will be illustrated and discussed.

Throughout the chapter, it will be assumed that in the field of agro-food marketing there are two types of products with very different characteristics: (1) the first group refers to fresh products, and includes fruits, vegetables, meat, and fish among others, which are minimally manipulated; and, (2) the second group, which consists of manufactured products, which have been processed and generally packaged at the agro-food industry. This classification is due to the fact that the product attributes or characteristics that consumers perceive in each case are different. For instance, there are attributes barely considered for fresh products, such as the brand, the label or packaging. In contrast, for manufactured products these attributes are more visible than, or at least as visible as, the product itself.

3.2 The sense of sight and the perception

What we perceived by our eyes influence our behaviour as consumers

The markets are places where the consumers find plenty of products and make their choices to satisfy their needs or wishes. Marketing, as a philosophy and organizational strategy, is focused on achieving customers' satisfaction and the search of information to take the most appropriate purchase actions. In this context, it is necessary to understand how consumers accomplish their choice of goods, especially food. The study of consumer behaviour deals with all of the ways people may act in their role as consumers (Schiffman and Kanuk, 1991). One of the most important tasks is the study of the determinants of behaviour, because if these variables and their performance are not identified, it will be difficult to meet the target segment conveniently. Food choice is often more influenced by the psychological interpretation of product properties than by its real physical properties (Rozin *et al.*, 1986).

One of the determinants of consumer behaviour is the perception. Classical authors differentiate between sensation and perception, but from the information processing perspective they are considered as a part of the same process, the perceptual process, whose main function is to extract information (Añaños *et al.*, 2009). The field of perception is concerned with explaining the operation of the senses and the experiences and behaviours resulting from their stimulation (Goldstein, 2009). Baptista *et al.* (2010) defined perception as the process by which an individual selects, organizes, and interprets stimuli to understand the world in a coherent and meaningful way. These stimuli can emerge from inside or outside the individual. The first refers to factors that denote a previous experience, such as predisposition, motivations, attitudes, etc. The latter are perceived by the senses, that is, they can be seen, smelt, touched, etc. In the brain, signals from the individual sensory streams are processed simultaneously in a modality-specific fashion to create a sensory representation of the external world (Thesen *et al.*, 2004).

Sensory marketing is an application of the understanding of the sensations and perceptions into the field of marketing, this is, into consumer perception, cognition, emotion, learning, preference, choice, or evaluation. Krishna (2012) provides a conceptual framework for the field of sensory marketing (Figure 3.1).

It is the visible that has the greatest impact on us. In marketing, sight sense represents one of the most important study elements. It has a fundamental role in the recognition and memory of the image, advertising, packaging, products, symbols, brands, logos, location, and so on. All of them have been treated very seriously to affect consumers' perception of products (Baptista *et al.*, 2010).

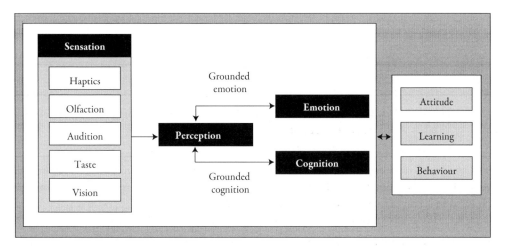

Figure 3.1. A conceptual framework of sensory marketing (adapted from Krishna, 2012).

3.3 Attributes perceived by the sense of sight

A product is made of a wide sort of components that can make it unique, such as design, style, colour, shape, size, packaging, and so on. Consumers' preferences and attitudes are determined by different characteristics of the products; many of them are perceived through the sense of sight. Next, it will be discussed the influence of visual food properties on the product perception and how they may affect the consumers' buying decisions.

3.3.1 Colour

> Colour choice is essential in food marketing. A wrong decision may compromise the future of the company

Colour is the key property allowing us to distinguish one product from another (Pérez, 2014). As a concept, it has been defined many times and from many different viewpoints. From the standpoint of marketing, food colour can be considered as perhaps the single most important product-intrinsic sensory cue governing the sensory and hedonic expectations that the consumer holds concerning the foods and drinks that they want to purchase, and which they may subsequently consume (Spence, 2015).

Colours are a component of nonverbal signs, which are studied as one of the important market phenomena (Kotler and Keller, 2006; McWilliam, 1997). To consumers it is a very important feature, even without being directly related to the functional characteristics of the product. Singh (2006) revealed that around 60 to 90% of the appraisal is driven exclusively by colours. Sewall (1978) said that colour is one of the basic things, which have a psychological impact on consumers' mind and as a result on its buying behaviour. Colour is a central element of products, services, packages, logos, displays, and collaterals which influences perceptions (Aslam, 2006). It is a highly noticeable attribute for presenting images. It improves recognition, memory and increases subjects' attention (Wichmann, *et al.*, 2002). It is an important marketing communication tool, a memorable visual element and carries key symbolic and associative information about products (Garber *et al.*, 2000).

The functionality of a product is not the only feature that makes it attractive to the consumer, but also its ability to satisfy emotional, sensual, and personal needs. It is legendary the Henry Ford's mistake when ignoring consumer preferences for different colours at selling his Ford T. His sentence 'any customer can have a car painted any colour that he wants so long as it is black', included in his biography (Ford and Crowther, 2005), reflects a mistake in not taking into account the emotions that this product attribute conveys to the consumer. Another great American car maker, General Motors, took advantage from Fords' mistake. If colour is so important in purchasing a car, it is even more important in food products, because in addition to emotions, colour may be also a reflection of freshness, state of ripening, or product variety (Murakoshi *et al.*, 2013).

Colour can be distinguished in hue, brightness, and saturation. Valdez and Mehrabian (1994) explained the levels of these colour components. In hue, it can be distinguished between warm colours, with long wavelengths and cool colours, with short wavelengths. Cool colours were associated with calm, serene, and comfortable moods. In contrast, warm colours were associated with stressful and exciting moods (Wexner, 1954). Long-wavelength colours were more arousing than short-wavelength colours (Valdez and Mehrabian, 1994). Regarding brightness, there are light colours, that have much light reflection and dark colours with low light reflection. Hemphill (1996) proved that bright colours are associated with positive feelings, such as happiness, joy, and hope. Brighter colours are judged as being friendlier, more cultured, pleasant and beautiful. In contrast, dark colours can evoke negative feelings, such as boredom and sadness (Camgöz *et al.*, 2002). Finally, saturation allows us to differentiate between high in pure colours and low, in pale, greyish colour.

Colour affects every moment in life. How humans are affected by colours has obviously a psychological nature which indirectly influences norms, reactions, and individual behaviour. Colours in marketing directly affect the consumer behaviour and the effects of colours determine the behaviour of many consumers (Babolhavaeji *et al.*, 2015), it has even been noted as one of the determinants of children's Neophobia (Lafraire *et al.*, 2016). Although Piqueras-Fiszman and Spence (2014) show conflicting results in their review of the colour influence on the acceptance of foods, many authors found a positive relationship between these variables. Rolls *et al.* (1982) stated that people eat more candy if they are of different colours than if they are of a single colour, even if that is the consumer's favourite one. Later, Kahn and Wansink (2004) reached a similar conclusion also with candies and recently Geier *et al.* (2012) with potato chips.

Colour experiences vary from individual to individual, and it is not possible to know how another person experiences colour. One person's experience of a red shade can be perceived differently from another person (Singh, 2006). In spite of this, several works collected different meanings of colours as a transmitter of sensations, emotions, and images in general. Global managers need to recognize that the different meanings associated with specific colours may facilitate multi-segment marketing opportunities. The wrong colour choice can have negative impact on the image of the product and the company. Table 3.1 presents the meaning of the colours in the Western world (Singh, 2006). The table is adapted from Babolhavaeji *et al.* (2015) and Scott-Kemmis (2013).

As mentioned before, the meaning of colour for consumers is not uniform and varies depending on many factors: gender, age, education, the culture we grew up in, preconceived colour beliefs of the societies we live in, childhood associations with certain colours, and life experiences, whether those associations are negative or positive (Scott-Kemmis, 2013).

According to Singh (2006) there are differences in the perception of colours between genders. Khouw (2002) found that men were more tolerant to grey, white or black than women, and that combinations of red and blue creates confusion and distraction, with higher frequency of these reactions in women than men. In a study among Chinese consumers, Zhang (2015) found that red, orange, blue, black, and white colours are perceived as more masculine (than feminine), and that high levels of brightness tend to increase femininity – a result that was significant for the hue purple.

With respect to age, children might show more visual dominance (that is, simply relying on what they see) because they have not yet learned to integrate their senses in an adult-like manner (Gori *et al.*, 2008). Following Singh (2006), yellow is one of the most popular colours among the 5-12 year olds. In older people, some researchers (Phiplipsen *et al.*, 1995; Tepper, 1993) have been able to demonstrate more pronounced psychological effects of food colouring in older adults. The meaning of colours can be a result of learned associations, for example red, orange and green colours on traffic lights. Philipsen *et al.* (1995) stated that older people are more affected by colour in their perception of sweet taste than young people. Second, the meaning of colours can be determined by nature (i.e. associations between black and death) (Elliot and Maier, 2007). In foods, for example, blue colour was

Table 3.1. Colours, meanings and effects.

Colour	Represent	Effects
Red	energy; action; desire; love; passion	stimulating; exciting and motivating; attention-getting; assertive and aggressive
Orange	adventure and risk taking; social communication and interaction; friendship; divorce	enthusiasm; rejuvenation; stimulation; courage; vitality; fun; playful
Yellow	mind and intellect; happiness and fun; communication of new ideas	creative; quick decisions; anxiety producing; critical; non-emotional; light; warmth; motivation
Green	harmony and balance; growth; hope; wealth; health; prestige; serenity	rejuvenation; nurturing; dependable, agreeable and diplomatic; possessiveness; envy
Blue	communication; peace and calm; honesty; authority; religion; wisdom	conservative; predictable; orderly; rigid; trustworthy; dependable; secure; responsible
Purple/violet	inspiration; imagination; individuality; spirituality; royalty; sophistication; nostalgia; mystery; spirituality	empathy; controlled emotion; respectable and distinguished; impractical; immature; dignity; cynical
Pink	unconditional love; compassion; nurturing; hope; girlish	calming; non-threatening; affectionate; caring; immature
Brown	stability; structure; security; natural and wholesome; earth-like	comforting; protective; materialistic; simplistic; durable
Grey	neutrality; compromise; control	indecision; detached; depression; unemotional
White	innocence and purity; new beginning; equality and unity; fairness	impartial; rescuer; futuristic; efficient; clean; soft; noble
Black	mystery; power and control; prestige; value; timelessness; sophistication	formal, dignified and sophisticated; depressing; pessimistic

traditionally considered unacceptable to a majority of consumers (Cheskin, 1957; Hine, 1995). Nowadays, many foods are blue although they are directed to young consumers (Garber *et al.*, 2001, 2015).

Tofle *et al.* (2004) also argued that emotional reactions evoked by colour are a result of learned associations based on culture and characteristics of an individual. In this way, the meanings associated with colours vary from culture to culture (Babolhavaeji *et al.*, 2015). People perception of colours is based on the relationships between the colour and its associated meaning (Krietler and Krietler, 2001). Singh (2006) made a short revision about the relationship between colour and culture, where he showed that blue is the most preferred colour and black has a negative connotation, in general, across cultures. Different colours are sacred across cultures: green for Muslims, green was also sacred for Celtics until the Christian church introduced the white colour, orange in Hindu religion in India or red and white combination in Melanesia. In this sense, Shankar *et al.* (2010) in their study with coloured drinks in two different countries (UK and Taiwan) found that the expected flavours were different depending on the culture.

Moreover, the previous experience of individuals also affects colour perception and the influence of this feature in buying behaviour. For example, Parr *et al.* (2003) revealed that wine colour had a greater influence when the assessment was made by product experts than by social drinkers, even Oenology students from Bordeaux were cheated in their perception when the colour of the wine to be evaluated was modified (Morrot *et al.*, 2001).

Finally, environmental colour also has influence on mood, feelings and finally on consumer behaviour. For example, Scott (1931) investigated the effect of environmental colour on the behaviour of children, and reported that the presence of an undesired, distasteful or offensive colour may change child's mood and disposition from contentment to discontentment, from happiness to misery, all of which affects its nutrition. Although, colour is related to feelings about retail environment (Bellizzi *et al.*, 1983), it also affects distraction (Gerard, 1957) and influences anxiety (Jacobs and Suess, 1975). In a blue shopping environment, compared to a red one, people were more willing to look around and buy products. Other authors also reported that a blue environment was less distracting and also less purchasing decisions are postponed and more money was spent (Bellizzi *et al.* 1983; Bellizzi and Hite, 1992). Stroebele *et al.* (2004) make a review on the effect of environment on food intake. Retailers have traditionally used colour to project an image or to create a desired atmosphere. Warm colours tend to be physically stimulating, whereas cool colours seem to be more relaxing (Bellizzi *et al.*, 1983). For instance, the red colour seems to arouse and activate people by influencing the autonomic nervous system and certain brain areas; however, this influence may vary across cultures. For example, Chebat and Morrin (2007) found that French-Canadians had higher perceptions of product quality when the store exhibited a warm colour *décor*. In contrast, Anglo-Canadians had higher perceptions of product quality when the retail environment exhibited a cool colour *décor*.

Focusing on foods, colour is certainly a quality that defines them (Figure 3.2). Consumers associate colours to certain characteristics of the products (Aghdaie and Honari, 2014;

Ares and Deliza, 2010). Thus, fresh products, that is, those that have not been processed are associated with certain characteristics. The red fruits are associated with antioxidant activity; red meat with its high iron content; the green colour of vegetables with healthy characteristics; bluefish, for its richness in omega 3, etc. Borgogno *et al.* (2015), in their study on meat, have identified colour as one of the intrinsic quality cues strongly associated with customers' expectations while shopping. The colour is also used as an indicator of maturation of a fresh vegetal product. For example, green bananas are assumed not to be ripe and ready to eat, whereas yellow bananas are perceived as better tasting and more appealing, and brown coloured bananas are discarded and not eaten because they are not seen as fresh (e.g. Elliot, 2012, mentioned by Lotz, 2016).

Colour is so relevant that a colour is often added to certain foods to enhance a feature or associate the colour with some feeling. It is a traditional practice that already took place in ancient Egypt, where candy makers around 1500 BC added natural extracts and wine to improve products' appearance (Meggos, 1995). In the late nineteenth century, the dispute

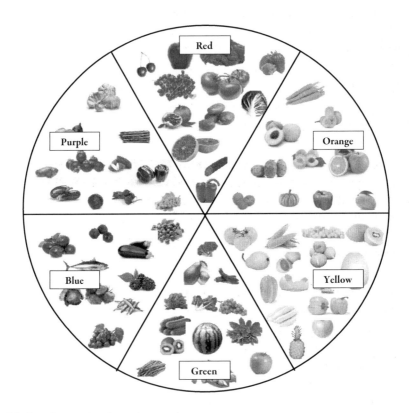

Figure 3.2. Food grouping by colour.

between butter and margarine manufacturers had colour as the focus point. The first fought for margarine manufacturers was about not adding colouring to improve the appearance of the product, and in some states of America passed laws that margarine be dyed an unappealing pink colour (Young, 2002). The addition of certain colours can increase the perception of health in products that are considered already healthy, but not in those that are not (Ruumpol, 2014). In yogurts or fruit juices, it is a common practice for the food industry to add dyes that although do not provide functional benefits to the product, relate it with the fruit.

One of the major factors affecting consumer perception is the type of colour which is used in packaging (Javed and Javed, 2015). In fact, it is the colour that attracts consumer attention in the first place, although the colours accepted by consumers in packaging are limited (Behnoud, 2012). Colours on packaging may cause apprehension and even rejection by customers (Prinsloo *et al.*, 2012); therefore, packaging colours may cause strategic failure if they are not properly chosen (Aslam, 2006).

Labrecque and Milne (2012) showed that colours can be used strategically to influence buying intentions, personality, and congeniality of a brand. In this sense, Funk and Ndubisi (2006) have stressed that colours can arouse the interest in a product and can motivate customers toward its buying. Like a carefully chosen brand name, colour carries intrinsic meaning that becomes central to the brand's identity, contributes to brand recognition (Abril *et al.*, 2009), and communicates the desired image of the company or product (Bottomley and Doyle, 2006).

Garber *et al.* (2001) discussed different strategies for companies when choosing a new packaging colour. On one hand, it consists of using colours traditionally associated with the product itself, such as green for mint or brown for cola; the second strategy consists of using new colours not directly related to the product as a tool to surprise the consumer and get their attention, and the third, cutting the relationship between colour and the product, making the container opaque or little identifiable with the colour of the product.

Companies choose colours for their logos or packages as an element of identification and differentiation, and often seek that consumers relate the company with a certain emotion linked to a colour (Figure 3.3). Coca-Cola seeks with its red colour transmitting happiness. Orange reflects excitement and enthusiasm, and demands attention in a similar way as red, but it is less aggressive (because red is also associated with danger). Hence, orange is the choice of brands targeting children, such as Fanta. The yellow colour is associated with joy, happiness and stimulates appetite. Well-known brands, such as McDonalds, have chosen yellow for their logo. Green is associated with natural and healthy products (Schuldt, 2013).

For example, Activia has chosen green to emphasize the image of healthy product. This also explains why McDonald's leave his mythical red base in its logo in favour of the green, in an attempt to reposition its brand towards healthy food and sustainable lifestyle.

In many cases, companies have achieved a direct association between the colour and the brand and sometimes the solely reference to the colour can distinguish them from the rest. The importance of colour as a tool for differentiation is so high that Cadbury and Nestle have been involved for years in a dispute on the use of the violet colour on the packaging of their chocolates (O'Connor, 2011). Some companies have tried to use colour as a tool to encourage consumption (Kahn and Wansink, 2004; Rolls *et al.*, 1982). Thus, M & M or Haribo use a wide variety of colours in their products to make them more attractive to consumers.

Sometimes, companies have been forced to change the colour of the product or packaging, either because consumers expect to find another flavour when tasted the product, the product was considered unnatural, or because the brand identity was lost. For example, Pepsi,

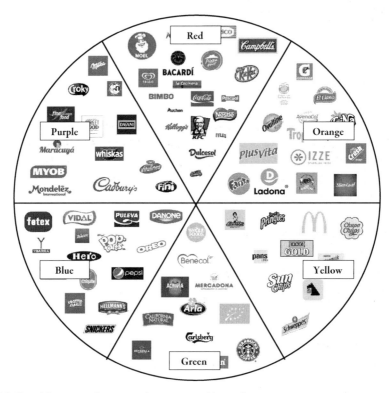

Figure 3.3. Food logos and companies grouped by colour.

few years ago, launched a new drink 'Pepsi crystal', in which the only difference with its cola drink was the transparent colour. The market response to this innovation was negative, as consumers preferred the classic brown colour. In a unique sign of innovation, Heinz, the world famous manufacturer of ketchup, launched this product with containers of different colours, thinking that the experience with food would be different and more fun. However, the product failed miserably and returned to red, also highlighting the naturalness of that colour for the tomato sauce.

Another example involves Coca-Cola and its different types of cola drink. Each type has a different colour match (red for regular coke, silver for light coke, and black for zero coke), and the company had different can colours for each type of cola. However, during 2015 in some countries, such as Spain, they have been forced to change all cans back to the traditional red colour, with the aim of unifying their brand identity and relate all their products with the colour of happiness.

In short, colour is essential in food marketing, and it is almost as vital as the product itself: it contributes largely to create the image of the product; it has been a source of major dispute between brands, as well as a source of important failures at product launch or positioning.

3.3.2 Shape

The importance of shape in food marketing: you love it or hate it

Shape is another important marketing tool, both in fresh and manufactured products. For fresh food, shape is an inherent feature of fruit and vegetables and consumers expect regularity. For packaged food, shape can communicate different emotions, and is also an indicator of consumers' sensory and hedonic expectations. As with colour, it can be the reason of remarkable market successes or failures.

Shape is one of the essential characteristics of objects grasped by the eyes. It refers to the spatial aspects of things, excepting location and orientation (Arnheim, 1954). There are several basic shapes and, as happens with colour, almost all of them have some characteristics associated. The book by Dreyfuss (1972) provides a deeper insight in the meaning of the various symbols.

In the field under examination, many fresh foods have a shape that is clearly identified by the consumer: oranges, apples, plums, peaches, watermelon, melon, and other fruits are round, while bananas, carrots, cucumbers or zucchini are elongated. Any change would result in a defect in quality standards and regularity denotes high quality. There have been attempts to develop varieties with a deviation in this parameter, as in the square watermelons, but they are mere anecdotes, which have only served to generate trivial news.

With manufactured products the situation is quite different, because the shape can be chosen according to the specific consumer needs and tastes. It is possible to find candies, pasta, cookies, etc. with many different shapes readily available in the marketplace. Sometimes, the choice of shape by the manufacturer is conditioned by the different features that they seek in the product, as sponginess or crispness, but sometimes, it is only an attribute with an aesthetic value. One might think that these products with specific shapes are targeted only for children, because the shape of a particular animal or their favourite cartoon can be an incentive for them to eat the food (Bergamaschi *et al.*, 2016), but children are not the only ones who consider this attribute; in products targeted to adults, different product shapes are also made in response to their preferences.

The physical form or design of a product is an unquestioned determinant of its marketplace success. A good design attracts consumers to a product, communicates to them, and adds value to the product by increasing the quality of the usage experiences associated with it (Bloch, 1995).

The form or design of a product may contribute to its success in several ways. Bloch (1995) developed a conceptual model and several propositions that relate the form of a product to consumer's psychological and behavioural responses. First, in cluttered markets, product form is one way to gain consumer notice. Second, the form or exterior appearance of a product is important as a mean of communicating information to consumers. Third, in addition to managerial considerations, product form is also significant in a larger sense because it affects the quality of our lives. The perception and usage of beautifully designed products may provide sensory pleasure and stimulation to the consumers.

Shapes' influence on purchase intention has been examined from different perspectives in the marketing literature. Ares and Deliza (2010) conducted a study to analyse the influence of package shape (and colour) on consumer expectations of a milk dessert. Two shapes (round and squared) were considered in the study. Conjoint analysis showed that round shape showed a highly significant higher utility than the square one when expected liking was considered, but no significant differences were found between these features for willingness to purchase. When the results of a word association task were considered, the round packages tended to be more associated with runny, creamy, and soft desserts; whereas, squared packages were associated with thick, and low-calorie milk desserts. These results suggested that package shape affected consumers' sensory and hedonic expectations of the desserts. This might indicate that package shape created sensory expectations regarding the texture of the desserts.

In other studies, shape angularity and potential perceptions have been related. For instance, Arnheim (1954) argued that angular shapes presented a confrontation between stimulus and surroundings, and are, therefore, readily perceived as expressive of confrontation or conflict. Similarly, Berlyne (1976) showed that angular shapes tended to induce associations with traits that express energy, toughness, and strength, whereas rounded shapes tended to induce perceptions of approachability, friendliness, and harmony. A similar consideration can be made for logos: Zhang *et al.* (2006) showed that rounded logos are readily perceived as harmonious and gentle, whereas angular logos trigger associations with conflict and aggressiveness.

The study by Yang and Raghubir (2005) showed that more elongated (taller) containers of a frequently purchased packaged good (beer), are perceived to contain a higher volume than less elongated (shorter) containers of an equivalent volume. They also found that purchase quantities are higher when cans are purchased, as compared to bottles. Within each of these package shapes, purchase quantities are higher for shorter bottles (cans) than they are for taller bottles and cans. Further, consumers who purchase both of them, purchase fewer bottles than cans.

Product functionality has also been related with shape. For example, the slim pack models were related to more user-friendly packaging, and these packs were assigned attributes such as comfortable and practical, while the blister pack designs were perceived to be more resistant (Rebollar *et al.*, 2012).

Product and/or packaging shape have been used in many occasions as a differentiation tool. Sometimes, food companies have modified this attribute to increase functionality, other times with the aim of relating the package with the product from which it is originated, and in other cases simply to attract consumer's attention or relating it with a specific sense. Various products are easily identified by their special shape, and have even led the pioneer company to the top of the market; for example, the Haribo bears, or Chupachups lollipop, the Filipinos, the Pringles chips, and many others. In the case of packaging, it is worth mentioning the case of SOSO Factory, a company dedicated primarily to the commercialization of sea salt in a minimalist distinctive egg-shaped container. In this case, not only the name evokes the product (in Spanish *soso* means the absence of salt), but the shape chosen (an egg) is the main product to which salt is added in Spain (there is even a popular saying that says 'it's duller than a non-salted egg', term used to refer to someone who is boring).

In other cases, some products have failed because they have been launched with an unsuitable packaging for a specific product category, because this type of packaging is related to other product category and they are not properly understood by consumers. It was the case of the mayonnaise and ketchup that were launched in tubes similar to those used for toothpaste. It had to be withdrawn from the market because the consumer did not accept them. Or the Filipinos' 'holes' that were not accepted either by consumers who preferred the traditional shape of these cookies.

As with colour, some companies have decided to change their package shape to innovate or get some other goal and have failed in the attempt, having to return to the original design. This was the case of Coca-Cola that, in an attempt to modernize its image, tried to change the shape of its classic bottle of 250 mL and had to return to the original format. For others, a change in the shape meant a success, for example, the company of cava Juve & Camps, changed the shape of its bottles and got that consumers related the product with a more traditional and with a higher quality image.

3.3.3 Size

In food, size does matter

Size is an important attribute in purchase decision, both in fresh and packaged food. One important line of research has dealt with the relationship between package size and eating behaviour, especially with the satiety perception. Size is also a communication tool that can be used to introduce new product in new markets or to indicate a good deal, such as in the case of generics. It is essential to adapt food size to the consumer segment needs.

In fresh fruits and horticultural products size is a dominant factor in determining wholesale and retail value, and it has been one of the key quality attributes for fruit industries (Jaeger et al., 2011). The value that consumers place on fruit and vegetable size depends on the specific fruit/vegetable category. For example, Bruhn (1995) found that for peaches and nectarines, very few consumers preferred smaller sized fruit and those who purchased small prebagged fruit, believed they were of low quality. In the study by Campbell et al. (2004) with satsuma mandarins, fruit size had a relative importance of 13.9%, somewhat lower than price (16.6%), blemish (16.6%) and colour (15.7%), but superior to type of the production or region of origin. In the study by Poole et al. (2007) also with mandarins, the fruit size was considered important or very important in the purchase decision for 50% of participants. However, Jaeger et al. (2011) found that size was of little importance in determining purchase likelihood/choice probability for kiwifruit.

Turning to packaged food, packaging size has been stressed as one important variable of packaging convenience (Draskovic, 2010). In the study by Koutsimanis *et al.* (2012) with cherry tomatoes, the package size was one of the three most important attributes, together with price and shelf life.

Recent studies have revealed that package and portion size have a great impact on food consumption. Raghubir and Greenleaf (2006) found that a small difference in the ratio of the sides of a rectangular invitation can affect the product perceptions, as well as its relative preferences and purchase intention. Purchase intentions were higher when information was presented in a rectangle with the golden ratio (1.62:1) as compared to the ratio of 1.38:1. They also found that the ratios of the dimensions of a product's box are related to its market share for frequently purchased supermarket products that are sold to consumers in boxes (such as cookies, cereals, soaps or detergents).

Narumi *et al.* (2012) determined that the apparent size of food can change the perception of satiety. In the same line, Rolls *et al.* (2002) showed that a larger portion size of an amorphous food (e.g. macaroni and cheese) significantly leads to greater food consumption. They have also shown that intake of a packaged snack is directly influenced by the size of the package, even if the total amount of the snack in the package is not visible. Furthermore, increased food consumption from bigger packages is not compensated at the next meal (Roll *et al.*, 2004). People learnt the relationship between package and portion size and developed a psychological constraint influencing the appropriate amount of food to be consumed (Birch *et al.*, 2000; Folkes *et al.*, 1993; Wansink, 1996).

The volume of food eaten tends to be a better indicator of how full individuals reported they felt than did the calorie density of the food (Rolls *et al.*, 1998, 2000, 2002).

The apparent volume of a food container also influences eating behaviour, and the apparent food volume is also assessed according to the size of the neighbouring objects (Coren, 1971). For instance, Wansink *et al.* (2005) showed that a larger serving bowl and serving spoon size (Wansink *et al.*, 2006) increased food consumption. On the contrary, Mishra *et al.* (2012) suggested that the size of cutlery may only work as an external cue in familiar settings.

There is overwhelming evidence that the size of food packaging and portions has steadily increased over the past 30 years (Rolls, 1986; Young and Nestle, 2002). Although this is a trend in much of the developed world, it is particularly common in the United States of Amercia, where the size of packages and portions are much larger (Rozin *et al.*, 2003). This factor may contribute to weight gain in some individuals (Hannum *et al.*, 2004; Nestle, 2002), because it is well supported that the size of a package can increase consumption

(Wansink, 1996). The same relationship has been observed with the size of portion servings in kitchens (Nisbett, 1968; Rolls *et al.*, 2002) and in restaurants (Edelman *et al.*, 1986), even of unfavourable food. The size of the package can have more influence than taste in determining ingested amounts (Wansinks and Cheney, 2005).

The package size affects consumer judgment and decisions, but not always in easily to uncover ways (Silayoi and Speece, 2004). Different sizes also appeal to consumers with somewhat different involvement. For example, low price for some low involvement products, such as unbranded or 'generics', is made possible through cost savings created by reduced packaging and promotional expenses. Generics are usually packaged in larger sizes, which communicate to consumers who are specifically looking for good deals. Such consumers find the low price of the generics, in the right size of packaging, to offer excellent value for money (Prendergast and Marr, 1997). In addition, this could imply that when product quality is hard to determine, as with generics, the packaging size effect is stronger. In some cases, consumers said that larger containers were more appealing and attractive (Silayoi and Speece, 2004). In other cases, participants reported negative perceptions of disproportionately large packaging (Venter *et al.*, 2011). In the study by Silayoi and Speece, (2004), people responsible for home shopping preferred to buy products with the dimension that fit their family size. Elderly respondents from New Zealand also disapproved over- sized packages for small families (Duizer *et al.*, 2009).

Sometimes small sizes allow companies to introduce products into new markets, such as olive oil in countries where consumption is unusual. In a study conducted in the United Kingdom with olive oil (Martínez *et al.*, 2002), although participants were regular consumers of olive oil products, most of them purchased olive oil in smaller size bottles compared to other cooking oils. Small-sized containers were considered to fit better in the cupboard and to be easier to handle. However, participants agreed that under certain circumstances, such as large households, regular cooking, and an appropriate size-price relationship, larger containers were always a better value for money.

There are many examples of companies that fit the size of their products to the different needs of its target segments, either by family size or product uses, but sometimes resizing is an important differentiation tool, such as mini-Babybel cheese or Petit Suisse.

3.3.4 General appearance and interactions among visual attributes

The whole is more than the sum of its parts

The general appearance of products is built by the set of characteristics discussed above. The combination of colours, shapes, and sizes allow obtaining different appearances of products. Visual characteristics of the products could be a communication tool, when considering how to bring to mind identities and values (Hulten *et al.*, 2009).

In the case of fresh products, this appearance is often conditioned by the product variety. For example, if we look at Figure 3.4 and we want to define a tomato, we will have some difficulties, given that all products in and around the basket are in fact tomatoes.

The overall appearance is a quality of extraordinary importance for consumers. In many cases, products have characteristics that do not meet the standard values leading to serious consequences even for the survival of certain product varieties, with the consequent loss of

Figure 3.4. Tomatoes with different appearance (photo: Arantxa Alonso Sanchis).

biodiversity. When looking at fresh products in supermarkets, homogeneity is a constant fact. It goes so far that products with good organoleptic characteristics, with only a defect in appearance do not meet the supermarket lines requirements and are considered waste products. This represents an increase in food waste, one of the major current problems of the food chain. Nowadays, several awareness campaigns have been launched, both by public bodies and private companies so that consumers deem fit these products for consumption. It is remarkable the successful campaign conducted by Intermarché, called 'Fruits et Légumes Moche', which showed products with imperfections and distortions, packaged attractively and with a lower price. To enhance the effect of the campaign, they offered tastings of juices and soups prepared with the 'ugly' fruits and vegetables.

In manufactured products, the important role of the package, as an experience trigger, reinforces the need for a continuous renewal of design, form, colours, and texture (Hultén et al., 2009). Packaging and packaging design can contribute to competitive advantage for food marketing (Rundh, 2009).

The interrelationship between attributes that can be perceived by sight and altogether built the overall appearance of the product has also been studied. Ares and Deliza (2010) investigated the relationship between size and shape, establishing that the size of the serving was perceived differently for round and square packages. Consumers considered the serving of a square package as adequate, whereas the serving of a round package was regarded as small. Vertical-horizontal illusions can also influence consumers' preferences. People tend to focus on the vertical dimension at the expense of the horizontal dimension of a cylindrical object (Piaget, 1968). Wansink and Van Ittersum (2003) have shown that this basic visual bias can influence different sorts of people (teens, regular people, and bartenders) to pour and drink more juice or soda into short, wide glasses than into tall, narrow glasses that held the same volume.

3.4 Interactions between senses

The senses do not work as isolated systems. They interact and even can change the perception

Finally, it must be considered that the attributes perceived by sight can also influence the consumers' perceptions made through other senses.

Becker et al. (2011) found that an intense sensation in one modality (e.g. perceiving a packaging shape as powerful or potent) should lead to an intense sensation in another modality (e.g. the experience of a full, strong taste).

The interaction between the colour and the sense of taste has been one of the most studied ones. It is important to realize that the psychological effects of food colouring are not restricted to the sensory discriminative domain. It has often been suggested that food colouring can modulate certain of our food-related behaviours (Spence, 2015). Consumers will tend to expect that more intensely coloured foods and beverages (not to mention the packaging in which such products come) will have a more intense taste/flavour (Spence, 2015). For example, the colour intensity has influence on the perception of sweetness in various fruit-flavoured yoghurts (Calvo et al., 2001), in coloured sucrose solutions (Johnson and Clydesdale, 1982), in redness in strawberry-flavoured beverages (Johnson et al., 1983) or in colour in cherry-flavoured beverages (Johnson et al., 1982).

The majority of the research that has been published to date has convincingly demonstrated that food colour affects the ability of people to correctly identify the flavour of food and drink (Spence, 2015). This research has been conducted with vegetables (Urbányi, 1982), dairy products (Calvo et al., 2001; Wadhmani and McMahon, 2012), cakes (Dubose et al., 1980) or drinks (Zampini et al., 2007, 2008). In some cases, specific tastes are associated with specific colours. The red colour is strongly associated with sweetness and the green colour with sourness (Heiltjes, 2014); probably it is because of the relationship between colour and taste in fruits. Many fruits make as they ripen a transition from green to red through yellow notes (Lavin and Lawless, 1998; Maga, 1974; Zampini et al., 2007). As a consequence, the addition of a red colouring to food increases the perception of a sweet taste (Strugnell, 1997) and reduces the taste of bitterness (Maga, 1974).

Such effects can also be applied in packaging design to change product perception. For example, the taste of 7-Up was evaluated as lemonier in cans where 15% of yellow colour was added to the green, compared to the original green cans (Hine, 1995). However, it has been difficult to relate the saltiness with a specific colour (Maga, 1974), although Wan et al. (2014) found a relationship between this taste and white colour. Other authors have found a relationship between more intense colours and spicier (Shermer and Levitan, 2014) or sweeter (Clydesdale et al., 1992) flavours; thus, a possible strategy to reduce sugar content in foods and make them healthier without diminishing their acceptance, could be increasing the colour intensity.

Another relevant aspect is that food colours are not necessarily associated with just one taste/flavour (Zampini et al., 2007). Similar food colours may give rise to qualitatively different flavour expectations depending on the category of the product under consideration (for example, soft drinks, cakes, noodles, curry, and so on) and possibly also the brand (Piqueras-Fiszman and Spence, 2011). On the other hand, Hoegg and Alba (2007) experimented with the flavour and colour of orange juices, finding that consumers identified as the most similar juices in taste those with more similar colours. The expectations of taste, taking into account the colour of the products, are conditioned by previous experience of the consumer (Shankar *et al.*, 2010), by cultural differences or the origin of consumers (Shankar *et al.*, 2009) or personal characteristics of the individual connected with their capacity to perceive the taste. In this sense, Zampini *et al.* (2008) considered that there are several types of people depending on how 'well they perceive the taste': the 'supertasters' are less affected by the colour of a drink that 'medium tasters ', which in turn are less affected than the 'non-tasters.' Also consumer age affects the influence of colour on the perception of the flavour intensity (Chan and Kane-Martinelli, 1997; Zhou *et al.*, 2015.).

Other researchers have demonstrated that when the meaning of food colouring is misinterpreted (that is, when it sets the wrong sensory expectations), then, this can have an adverse effect on people's subsequent taste ratings (Yeomans *et al.*, 2008). These researchers found differences among three groups of consumers who tasted ice cream made with smoked salmon. The first group of consumers was not given any information and, therefore, expected a strawberry flavour, so they did not like it at all. In the other groups, some information about the product composition was provided and they liked it. These results demonstrated that the meaning of colour in food and drink can be altered simply by the description that it is given for a product or dish.

Conversely, for other authors, the psychological effects of either adding or changing the intensity of food colouring on the intensity of taste/flavour perception are not completely clear (Spence, 2015). Alley and Alley (1998) and Frank *et al.* (1989) considered that there is no clear relationship between colour and flavour, although there is with the aroma. To Koza *et al.* (2005), what is closely related to colour is the olfactory perception. In this sense, Lwin *et al.* (2010) showed how the sense of smell may increase the perception of the sense of sight, but not *vice versa*.

Other authors studied the relationship between the sense of sight and hearing (Russel, 2002) and others between the sense of sight and touch, with results proving the domain of vision on touch (Kinney and Luria, 1970; Krishna, 2006).

In this way, the works that relate shape and texture are also remarkable, such as the one by Ares and Deliza (2010), who found that differences in consumer associations due to differences in package shape were mainly related to sensory expectations about texture characteristics (e.g. runny and thick) and to specific dessert types (e.g. egg custard or low-calorie desserts). In this line, Rebollar *et al.* (2012) found that consumers associate the format of chewing gum packs with the gum's functional attributes and sensory attributes of texture.

The slim pack models generated consumer expectations of a soft, light chewing gum, while the blister packs and pill packs were perceived by respondents as being dense and crunchy.

Finally, it is important to know that the variety of qualities is determinant in food acceptance. There is a very large body of empirical evidence to support the claim that increased variety in terms of gustatory, olfactory, and/or oral-somatosensory attributes of a meal, or food selection, results in increased food consumption (Hetherington *et al.*, 2006; Kahn and Wansink, 2004; Sørensen *et al.*, 2003; Wadhera and Capaldi, 2014).

3.5 Conclusions

In view of the above, there is no doubt about the importance of the sense of sight in the perception and subsequent acceptance of food products. A detailed analysis of the attributes that can be assessed by sight has led us to understand why there are such variety of products in the market, and how companies are using sensory information to properly position their products. Indeed, many of the marketing strategies that companies develop are closely related with features that can be perceived by the sense of sight. The choice of colour packaging, logo, size or shape of the product or the packaging, are not decisions that companies can take randomly, because they will influence the success or failure of their products in the market.

Companies should keep in mind that these external attributes can be decisive in shaping the image of the product. So, if they want to project a natural image, green colour seems to be the most appropriate. If they want harmony or proximity, rounded containers will be more suitable than the angular or square shaped, which would be preferred when the desire is to project energy or hardness. These are just some examples that demonstrate the importance of sensory marketing in the success or failure of a product.

On the other hand, this chapter has shown the relationship between sensory marketing, specifically in regard to the sense of sight, and three of the major social challenges of the twenty-first century (the health of consumers, food waste, and conservation of biodiversity). Sensory marketing can help in addressing them in an efficient way. It seems that the apparent size of food can change the perception of satiety and eating behaviour, and, therefore, help to control weight in some individuals. This fact must be taken into account due to its direct consequences on the health of consumers, e.g. obesity. Authors have also highlighted how the colour can be used to influence the sense of taste and, therefore, to reduce the content of some undesirable ingredients making food healthier.

Moreover, the food industry and sensory marketing can also play an important role in improving global sustainability through the knowledge of the effect of attributes perceived by the sense of sight. If it is known that an irregular appearance, far from standardized patterns, can increase the rejection of certain products and that this rejection can lead to something as undesirable as food waste or loss of essential biodiversity, strategies to mitigate these undesirable effects should be planned.

Finally, authors would like to highlight that, in spite of the many investigations in this field, specially directed to understand the consumer, new lines of research should be opened to allow the food system to contribute to the improvement of society from different perspectives.

References

Abril, P.S., Olazábal, A.M. and Cava, A., 2009. Marketing and the law. Journal of the Academy of Marketing Science 37(3): 375-377.

Aghdaie, S.F.A. and Honari, R., 2014. Investigating the psychological impact of colours on process of consumer shopping behaviour. International Review of Management and Business Research 3(2): 1244.

Alley, R.L. and Alley, T.R., 1998. The influence of physical state and colour on perceived sweetness. Journal of Psychology 132(5): 561-568.

Añaños, E., Estaún, S., Tena, D., Mas, M.T. and Valli, A., 2009. Psicología y comunicación publicitaria. Universitat Autònoma de Barcelona, Barcelona, Spain, 151 pp.

Ares, G. and Deliza, R., 2010. Studying the influence of package shape and colour on consumer expectations of milk desserts using word association and conjoint analysis. Food Quality and Preference 21(8): 930-937.

Arnheim, R., 1954. Art and visual perception: a psychology of the creative eye. University of California Press, Berkeley, CA, USA, 508 pp.

Aslam, M.M., 2006. Are you selling the right colour? A cross-cultural review of colour as a marketing cue. Journal of Marketing Communications 12(1): 15-30.

Babolhavaeji, M., Vakilian, M.A. and Slambolchi, A., 2015. The role of product colour in consumer behaviour. Advanced Social Humanities and Management 2(1): 9-15.

Baptista, M.V., Del Fátima León, M. and Mora, C., 2010. Neuromarketing: conocer al paciente por sus percepciones. Tec Empresarial 4(3): 9-19.

Becker, L., Van Rompay, T.J., Schifferstein, H.N. and Galetzka, M., 2011. Tough package, strong taste: the influence of packaging design on taste impressions and product evaluations. Food Quality and Preference 22(1): 17-23.

Behnood, K., 2012. Fachkräfte gewinnen für kleine und mittlere Unternehmen: Employer Branding leicht gemacht. In: Aghdaie, S.F.A. and Honari, R. (eds.) Investigating the psychological impact of colors on process of consumer shopping behavior. International Review of Management and Business Research 3(2): 1244.

Bellizzi, J.A. and Hite, R.E., 1992. Environmental colour, consumer feelings, and purchase likelihood. Psychology and Marketing 9(5): 347-363.

Bellizzi, J.A., Crowley, A.E. and Hasty, R.W., 1983. Reducing assortment: an attribute-based approach. Journal of Marketing 65: 50-63.

Bergamaschi, V., Olsen, A., Laureati, M., Zangenberg, S., Pagliarini, E. and Bredie, W.L., 2016. Variety in snack servings as determinant for acceptance in school children. Appetite 96: 628-635.

Berlyne, D.E., 1976. The affective significance of uncertainty. In: Serban, G. (ed.) Psychopathology of human adaptation. Springer, New York, NY, USA, pp. 319-341.

Birch, L.L., Engell, D. and Rolls, B.J., 2000. Serving portion size influences 5-year-old but not 3-year-old children's food intakes. Journal of the American Dietetic Association 100: 232-234.

Bloch, P.H., 1995. Seeking the ideal form: product design and consumer response. Journal of Marketing 59(3): 16-29.

Borgogno, M., Favotto, S., Corazzin, M., Cardello, A.V. and Piasentier, E., 2015. The role of product familiarity and consumer involvement on liking and perceptions of fresh meat. Food Quality and Preference 44: 139-147.

Bottomley, P.A. and Doyle, J.R., 2006. The interactive effects of colours and products on perceptions of brand logo appropriateness. Marketing Theory 6(1): 63-83.

Bruhn, C.M., 1995. Consumer and retailer satisfaction with the quality and size of California peaches and nectarines. Journal of Food Quality 18(3): 241-256.

Calvo, C., Salvador, A. and Fiszman, S.M., 2001. Influence of colour intensity on the perception of colour and sweetness in various fruit-flavoured yoghurts. European Food Research and Technology 213(2): 99-103.

Camgöz, N., Yener, C. and Güvenç, D., 2002. Effects of hue, saturation, and brightness on preference. Colour Research and Application 27(3): 199-207.

Campbell, B.L., Nelson, R.G., Ebel, R.C., Dozier, W.A., Adrian, J.L. and Hockema, B.R., 2004. Fruit quality characteristics that affect consumer preferences for satsuma mandarins. HortScience 39(7): 1664-1669.

Chan, M.M. and Kane-Martinelli, C., 1997. The effect of colour on perceived flavour intensity and acceptance of foods by young adults and elderly adults. Journal of the American Dietetic Association 97(6): 657-659.

Chebat, J.C. and Morrin, M., 2007. Colors and cultures: exploring the effects of mall décor on consumer perceptions. Journal of Business Research 60(3): 189-196.

Cheskin, L., 1957. How to predict what people will buy. Liveright Publishing Corporation, New York, NY, USA, 241 pp.

Clydesdale, F.M., Gover, R., Philipsen, D.H. and Fugardi, C., 1992. The effect of colour on thirst quenching, sweetness, acceptability and flavour intensity in fruit punch flavoured beverages. Journal of Food Quality 15(1): 19-38.

Coren, S., 1971. A size-contrast illusion without physical size differences. American Journal of Psychology 84(4): 565.

Draskovic, N., 2010. Packaging convenience. Consumer packaging feature or marketing tool? International Journal of Management Cases 12(2): 267-274.

Dreyfuss, H., 1972. Symbol sourcebook: an authoritative guide to international graphic symbols. McGraw-Hill, New York, NY, USA, 288 pp.

DuBose, C.N., Cardello, A.V. and Maller, O., 1980. Effects of colourants and flavourants on identification, perceived flavour intensity, and hedonic quality of fruit-flavoured beverages and cake. Journal of Food Science 45(5): 1393-1399.

Duizer, L.M., Roberson, T. and Han, J., 2009. Requirements for packaging from an ageing consumer's perspective. Packaging Technology and Science 22: 187-197.

Edelman, B., Engell, D., Bronstein, P. and Hirsch, E., 1986. Environmental effects on the intake of overweight and normal-weight men. Appetite 7(1): 71-83.

Elliott, C., 2012. Taste™: interrogating food, law, and color. The Senses and Society 7(3): 276-288.

Elliot, A.J. and Maier, M.A., 2007. Colour and psychological functioning. Current Directions in Psychological Science 16(5): 250-254.

Eurofound, 2013. Health and Wellbeing at work: a report on based on the fifth European Working conditions survey. Available at: http://tinyurl.com/mub5xet.

European Commission (EC), 2014. Towards a circular economy: a zero waste programme for Europe. Available at: http://tinyurl.com/mxucvam.

Folkes, V.S., Martin, I.M. and Gupta, K., 1993. When to say when: effects of supply on usage. Journal of Consumer Research 20(3): 467-477.

Ford, H. and Crowther, S., 2005. My life and work. 1st World Library. Fairfield, CT, USA, 324 pp.

Frank, R.A., Ducheny, K. and Mize, S.J.S., 1989. Strawberry odor, but not red colour, enhances the sweetness of sucrose solutions. Chemical Senses 14(3): 371-377.

Funk, D. and Ndubisi, N.O., 2006. Colour and product choice: a study of gender roles. Management Research News 29(1-2): 41-52.

Garber Jr., L.L., Hyatt, E.M. and Nafees, L., 2015. The effects of food colour on perceived flavour: a factorial investigation in India. Journal of Food Products Marketing 22(8): 1-20.

Garber Jr., L.L., Hyatt, E.M. and Starr Jr., R.G., 2000. The effects of food colour on perceived flavour. Journal of Marketing Theory and Practice 8(4): 59-72.

Garber Jr., L.L., Hyatt, E.M. and Starr Jr., R.G., 2001. Placing food colour experimentation into a valid consumer context. Journal of food products Marketing 7(3): 3-24.

Geier, A., Wansink, B. and Rozin, P., 2012. Red potato chips: segmentation cues can substantially decrease food intake. Health Psychology 31(3): 398-401.

Gerard, 1957. In: Singh, S. (2006). Impact of color on marketing. Management Decision 44(6): 783-789.

Goldstein, E.B., 2009. Encyclopedia of perception. SAGE Publications, Thousand Oaks, CA, USA, 1280 pp.

Gori, M., Del Viva, M., Sandini, G. and Burr, D.C., 2008. Young children do not integrate visual and haptic form information. Current Biology 18(9): 694-698.

Gustavsson, J., Cederberg, C. and Sonesson, U., 2011. Global food losses and food waste. Extent, causes and prevention. FAO, Rome, Italy.

Hannum, S.M., Carson, L., Evans, E.M., Canene, K.A., Petr, E.L., Bui, L. and Erdman, J.W., 2004. Use of portion-controlled entrees enhances weight loss in women. Obesity Research 12(3): 538-546.

Heiltjes, S., 2014. Touching brands: the effects of multisensory packaging design on brand and product perception and evaluation. Available at: http://tinyurl.com/jw2zumk.

Hekkert, P. and Schifferstein, H.N.J., 2008. Product experience. Elsevier, Amsterdam, the Netherlands.

Hemphill, M., 1996. A note on adults' color-emotion associations. Journal of Genetic Psychology 157: 275-281.

Hetherington, M.M., Foster, R., Newman, T., Anderson, A.S. and Norton, G., 2006. Understanding variety: tasting different foods delays satiation. Physiology and Behaviour 87(2): 263-271.

Hine, T., 1995. The total packaging: the secret history and hidden meanings of boxes, bottles, cans and other persuasive containers. Little Brown, New York, NY, USA.

Hoegg, J. and Alba, J.W., 2007. Taste perception: more than meets the tongue. Journal of Consumer Research 33(4): 490-498.

Hultén, B., Broweus, N. and Van Dijk, M., 2009. Sensory marketing. Palgrave Macmillan, Basingstoke, UK.

Jacobs, K.W. and Suess, J.F., 1975. Effects of four psychological primary colors on anxiety state. Perceptual and Motor Skills 41(1): 207-210.

Jaeger, S.R., Harker, R., Triggs, C.M., Gunson, A., Campbell, R.L., Jackman, R. and Requejo-Jackman, C., 2011. Determining consumer purchase intentions: the importance of dry matter, size, and price of kiwifruit. Journal of Food Science 76(3): S177-S184.

Javed, S.A. and Javed, S., 2015. The impact of product's packaging colour on customers' buying preferences under time pressure. Marketing and Branding Research 2(1): 4-14.

Johnson, J. and Clydesdale, F.M., 1982. Perceived sweetness and redness in coloured sucrose solutions. Journal of Food Science 47(3): 747-752.

Johnson, J.L., Dzendolet, E. and Clydesdale, F.M., 1983. Psychophysical relationship between sweetness and redness in strawberry-flavoured drinks. Journal of Food Protection 46(1): 21-25.

Johnson, J.L., Dzendolet, E., Damon, R., Sawyer, M. and Clydesdale, F.M., 1982. Psychophysical relationships between and colour in cherry-flavoured perceived sweetness beverages. Journal of Food Protection 45(7): 601-606.

Kahn, B.E. and Wansink, B., 2004. The influence of assortment structure on perceived variety and consumption quantities. Journal of Consumer Research 30(4): 519-533.

Khouw, N., 2002. The meaning of color for gender. Colors matters – Research. Available at: www.colormatters.com.

Kinney, J.A.S. and Luria, S.M., 1970. Conflicting visual and tactual-kinesthetic stimulation. Perception and Psychophysics 8(3): 189-192.

Kotler, P. and Keller, K.L., 2006. Marketing management. Prentice Hall International, Upper Saddle River, NJ, USA, 889 pp.

Kotler, P., Kartajaya, H. and Setiawan, I., 2010. Marketing 3.0: from products to customers to the human spirit. John Wiley and Sons, New York, NY, USA.

Koutsimanis, G., Getter, K., Behe, B., Harte, J. and Almenar, E., 2012. Influences of packaging attributes on consumer purchase decisions for fresh produce. Appetite 59(2): 270-280.

Koza, B.J., Cilmi, A., Dolese, M. and Zellner, D.A., 2005. Colour enhances orthonasal olfactory intensity and reduces retronasal olfactory intensity. Chemical Senses 30(8): 643-649.

Krietler and Krietler, 2001. In: Aghdaie, S.F.A. and Honari, R. (ed.) Investigating the psychological impact of colors on process of consumer shopping behavior. International Review of Management and Business Research 3(2): 1244.

Krishna, A., 2006. Interaction of senses: the effect of vision versus touch on the elongation bias. Journal of Consumer Research 32(4): 557-566.

Krishna, A., 2012. An integrative review of sensory marketing: Engaging the senses to affect perception, judgment and behaviour. Journal of Consumer Psychology 22(3): 332-351.

Labrecque, L.I. and Milne, G.R., 2012. Exciting red and competent blue: the importance of colour in marketing. Journal of Academy of Marketing Science 40(5): 711-727.

Lafraire, J., Rioux, C., Giboreau, A. and Picard, D., 2016. Food rejections in children: cognitive and social/environmental factors involved in food neophobia and picky/fussy eating behaviour. Appetite 96: 347-357.

Lavin, J. and Lawless, H., 1998. Effects of colour and odor on judgments of sweetness among children and adults. Food Quality and Preference 9: 283-289.

Lotz, R.N., 2016. Colour associations as advertising strategies: an analysis of consumer attitudes toward the healthfulness of energy bar packaging. Portland State University, University Honors theses, Paper 249, Portland, OR, USA.

Lwin, M., Morrin, M. and Krishna, A., 2010. Exploring the superadditive effects of scent and pictures on verbal recall: an extension of dual coding theory. Journal of Consumer Psychology 20: 317-326.

Maga, J.A., 1974. Influence of colour on taste thresholds. Chemical Senses and Flavour 1: 115-119.

Martínez, M.G., Aragonés, Z. and Poole, N., 2002. A repositioning strategy for olive oil in the UK market. Agribusiness 18(2): 163-180.

Martínez-Carrasco, L., Brugarolas, M., Martínez-Poveda, A., Ruiz, J.J. and García, S., 2015. Aceptación de variedades tradicionales de tomate en mercados locales. Un estudio de valoración contingente. ITEA 111(1): 56-72.

McWilliam, G., 1997. Low involvement brands: is the brand manager to blame? Marketing Intelligence and Planning 15: 60-70.

Meggos, H., 1995. Food colours: an international perspective. Manufacturing Confectioner 1995: 59-65.

Mishra, A., Mishra, H. and Masters, T.M., 2012. The influence of bite size on quantity of food consumed: a field study. Journal of Consumer Research 38(5): 791-795.

Morrot, G., Brochet, F. and Dubourdieu, D., 2001. The colour of odors. Brain Lang 79: 309-320.

Murakoshi, T., Masuda, T., Utsumi, K., Tsubota, K. and Wada, Y., 2013. Glossiness and perishable food quality: visual freshness judgment of fish eyes based on luminance distribution. PloS ONE 8(3): e58994.

Narumi, T., Ban, Y., Kajinami, T., Tanikawa, T. and Hirose, M., 2012. Augmented perception of satiety: controlling food consumption by changing apparent size of food with augmented reality. Proceedings of the SIGCHI Conference on Human Factors in Computing Systems, May 5-10, 2012. Austin, TX, USA, pp. 109-118.

Nestle, M., 2002. Food politics: how the food industry influences nutrition and health, Vol. 3. University of California Press, Berkeley, CA, USA, 534 pp.

Nisbett, R.E., 1968. Determinants of food intake in obesity. Science 159(3820): 1254-1255.

O'Connor, Z., 2011. Logo colour and differentiation: a new application of environmental colour mapping. Colour Research and Application 36(1): 55-60.

Parr, W.V., Geoffrey White, K. and Heatherbell, D.A., 2003. The nose knows: influence of colour on perception of wine aroma. Journal of Wine Research 14(2-3): 79-101.

Perez, E., 2014. Physical properties of matter. Understanding by design: complete collection. Paper 272. Available at: http://tinyurl.com/k5muzrl.

Pérez-Farinós, N., López Sobaler, A.M., Robledo de Dios, T., Dal Re Saavedra, M.A., Villar Villaba, C. and Ortega Anta, R.M., 2015. Contenido de sal en los alimentos en España. 2012. Agencia Española de Consumo, Seguridad Alimentaria y Nutrición. Ministerio de Sanidad, Servicios Sociales e Igualdad. Madrid, Spain, 2015.

Philipsen, D.H., Clydesdale, F.M., Griffin, R.W. and Stern, P., 1995. Consumer age affects response to sensory characteristics of a cherry flavoured beverage. Journal of Food Science 60(2): 364-368.

Piaget, J., 1968. Quantification, conservation, and nativism. Science 162(3857): 976-979.

Piqueras-Fiszman, B. and Spence, C., 2011. Crossmodal correspondences in product packaging. Assessing colour-flavour correspondences for potato chips (crisps). Appetite 57(3): 753-757.

Poole, N.D., Martínez-Carrasco, L. and Vidal, F., 2007. Quality perceptions under evolving information conditions: implications for diet, health and consumer satisfaction. Food Policy 32(2): 175-188.

Prendergast, G.P. and Marr, N.E., 1997. Generic products: who buys them and how do they perform relative to each other? European Journal of Marketing 31(2): 94-109.

Prinsloo, N., Van der Merwe, D., Bosman, M. and Erasmus, A.C., 2012. A critical review of the significance of food labelling during consumer decision making. Journal of Family Ecology and Consumer Sciences 40.

Raghubir, P. and Greenleaf, E.A., 2006. Ratios in proportion: what should the shape of the package be? Journal of Marketing 70(2): 95-107.

Rebollar, R., Lidón, I., Serrano, A., Martín, J. and Fernández, M.J., 2012. Influence of chewing gum packaging design on consumer expectation and willingness to buy. An analysis of functional, sensory and experience attributes. Food Quality and Preference 24(1): 162-170.

Rolls, B.J., 1986. Sensory-specific satiety. Nutrition Reviews 44(3): 93-101.

Rolls, B.J., Bell, E.A. and Waugh, B.A., 2000. Increasing the volume of a food by incorporating air affects satiety in men. American Journal of Clinical Nutrition 72(2): 361-368.

Rolls, B.J., Castellanos, V.H., Halford, J.C., Kilara, A., Panyam, D., Pelkman, C.L., Smith, G.P. and Thorwart, M.L., 1998. Volume of food consumed affects satiety in men. American Journal of Clinical Nutrition 67(6): 1170-1177.

Rolls, B.J., Morris, E.L. and Roe, L.S., 2002. Portion size of food affects energy intake in normal-weight and overweight men and women. American Journal of Clinical Nutrition 76(6): 1207-1213.

Rolls, B.J., Roe, L.S., Kral, T.V., Meengs, J.S. and Wall, D.E., 2004. Increasing the portion size of a packaged snack increases energy intake in men and women. Appetite 42(1): 63-69.

Rolls, B.J., Rowe, E.A. and Rolls, E.T., 1982. How sensory properties of foods affect human feeding behaviour. Physiology and Behaviour 29(3): 409-417.

Rozin, P., Kabnick, K., Pete, E., Fischler, C. and Shields, C., 2003. The ecology of eating smaller portion sizes in France than in the United States help explain the French paradox. Psychological Science 14(5): 450-454.

Rozin, P., Pelchat, M.L. and Fallon, A.E., 1986. Psychological factors influencing food choice'. In: Ritson, C., Gofton, L. and McKenzie, J. (eds.) The food consumer. John Wiley and Sons Ltd., New York, NY, USA, pp. 85-106.

Rundh, B., 2009. Packaging design: creating competitive advantage with product packaging. British Food Journal 111(9): 988-1002.

Russell, C.A., 2002. Investigating the effectiveness of product placements in television shows: the role of modality and plot connection congruence on brand memory and attitude. Journal of Consumer Research 29(3): 306-318.

Ruumpol, J.G., 2014. In the eye of the consumer: the influence of package shape and package colour on perceived product healthfulness. Available at: http://tinyurl.com/mymdhpb.

Schiffman, L.G. and Kanuk, L.L., 1991. Communication and consumer behavior. Consumer Behavior 2: 268-306.

Schuldt, J.P., 2013. Does green mean healthy? Nutrition label colour affects perceptions of healthfulness. Health Communication 28(8): 814-821.

Scott, G.D., 1931. The psychic value of music and color in infant and child nutrition. A.R. Elliott Pub. Co., London, UK.

Scott-Kemmis, J., 2013. Target markets – Using colour psychology to attract your target markets. Available at: http://tinyurl.com/brrrak9.

Sewall, M.A., 1978. Market segmentation based on consumer ratings of proposed product designs. Journal of Marketing Research 4(15): 557-564.

Shankar, M.U., Levitan, C. and Spence, C., 2010. Grape expectations: the role of cognitive influences in colour-flavour interactions. Consciousness and Cognition 19: 380-390.

Shankar, M.U., Levitan, C.A., Prescott, J. and Spence, C., 2009. The influence of colour and label information on flavour perception. Chemosensory Perception 2: 53-58.

Shermer, D.Z. and Levitan, C.A., 2014. Red hot: the cross modal effect of colour intensity on piquancy. Multisensory Research 27: 207-223.

Silayoi, P. and Speece, M., 2004. Packaging and purchase decisions: an exploratory study on the impact of involvement level and time pressure. British Food Journal 106(8): 607-628.

Singh, S., 2006. Impact of colour on marketing. Management Decision 44(6): 783-789.

Sørensen, L.B., Møller, P., Flint, A., Martens, M. and Raben, A., 2003. Effect of sensory perception of foods on appetite and food intake: a review of studies on humans. International Journal of Obesity 27(10): 1152-1166.

Spence, C., 2002. The ICI report on the secret of the senses. The Communication Group, London, UK.

Spence, Ch., 2015. On the psychological impact of food colour. Flavour 4: 21.

Stroebele, N. and De Castro, J.M., 2004. Effect of ambience on food intake and food choice. Nutrition 20(9): 821-838.

Strugnell, C., 1997. Colour and its role in sweetness perception. Appetite 28: 85.

Tepper, B.J., 1993. Effects of a slight color variation on consumer acceptance of orange juice. Journal of Sensory Studies 8(2): 145-154.

Thesen, T., Vibell, J.F., Calvert, G.A. and Österbauer, R.A., 2004. Neuroimaging of multisensory processing in vision, audition, touch, and olfaction. Cognitive Processing 5(2): 84-93.

Tofle, R.B., Schwartz, B., Yoon, S. and Max-Royale, A., 2004. Colour in healthcare environments: a critical review of the research literature. The Coalition for Health Environments Research (CHER), CA, USA.

Urbanyi, G., 1982. Investigation into the interaction of different properties in the course of sensory evaluation. I. The effect of colour upon the evaluation of taste in fruit and vegetable products. Acta Alimentaria 11: 233-243.

Valdez, P. and Mehrabian, A., 1994. Effects of colour on emotions. Journal of Experimental Psychology 123(4): 394-409.

Venter, K., Van der Merwe, D., De Beer, H., Kempen, E. and Bosman, M., 2011. Consumers' perceptions of food packaging: an exploratory investigation in Potchefstroom, South Africa. International Journal of Consumer Studies 35(3): 273-281.

Wadhera, D. and Capaldi-Phillips, E.D., 2014. A review of visual cues associated with food on food acceptance and consumption. Eating Behaviours 15(1): 132-143.

Wadhwani, R. and McMahon, D.J., 2012. Colour of low-fat cheese influences flavour perception and consumer liking. Journal of Dairy Science 95(5): 2336-2346.

Wan, X., Woods, A.T., Van den Bosch, J.J., McKenzie, K.J., Velasco, C. and Spence, C., 2014. Cross-cultural differences in crossmodal correspondences between basic tastes and visual features. Frontiers in Psychology 5: 1365.

Wansink, B., 1996. Can package size accelerate usage volume? Journal of Marketing 1-14.

Wansink, B. and Cheney, M.M., 2005. Super bowls: serving bowl size and food consumption. Journal of the American Medical Association 13:293(14): 1727-1728.

Wansink, B. and Van Ittersum, K., 2003. Bottoms up! The influence of elongation on pouring and consumption volume. Journal of Consumer Research 30(3): 455-463.

Wansink, B., Painter, J.E. and North, J., 2005. Bottomless bowls: why visual cues of portion size may influence intake. Obesity research 13(1): 93-100.

Wansink, B., Van Ittersum, K. and Painter, J.E., 2006. Ice cream illusions bowls, spoons, and self-served portion sizes. American Journal of Preventive Medicine 31(3): 240-243.

Wexner, L.B., 1954. The degree to which colours (hues) are associated with mood-tones. Journal of Applied Psychology 38: 432-435.

Wichmann, F.A., Sharpe, L.T. and Gegenfurtner, K.R., 2002. The contributions of colour to recognition memory for natural scenes. Journal of Experimental Psychology: Learning, Memory, and Cognition 28(3): 509.

World Health Organization (WHO), 2013. Plan de acción mundial para la prevención y el control de las enfermedades no transmisibles 2013-2020. Proyecto revisado y actualizado. Geneva, Switzerland.

Yang, S. and Raghubir, P., 2005. Can bottles speak volumes? The effect of package shape on how much to buy. Journal of Retailing 81(4): 269-281.

Yeomans, M.R., Chambers, L., Blumenthal, H. and Blake, A., 2008. The role of expectancy in sensory and hedonic evaluation: the case of smoked salmon ice-cream. Food quality and preference, 19(6): 565-573.

Young, A., 2002. The war on margarine. Foundation for Economic Education. Available at: https://fee.org/articles/the-war-on-margarine.

Young, L.R. and Nestle, M., 2002. The contribution of expanding portion sizes to the US obesity epidemic. American Journal of Public Health 92(2): 246-249.

Zampini, M., Sanabria, D., Phillips, N. and Spence, C., 2007. The multisensory perception of flavour: assessing the influence of colour cues on flavour discrimination responses. Food Quality and Preference 18(7): 975-984.

Zampini, M., Wantling, E., Phillips, N. and Spence, C., 2008. Multisensory flavour perception: assessing the influence of fruit acids and colour cues on the perception of fruit-flavoured beverages. Food Quality and Preference 19(3): 335-343.

Zhang, S., 2015. Colour associations with masculine and feminine brand personality among Chinese consumers. PhD-thesis, Concordia University, Montreal, QC, Canada.

Zhang, Y., Feick, L. and Price, L.J., 2006. The impact of self-construal on aesthetic preference for angular versus rounded shapes. Personality and Social Psychology Bulletin 32(6): 794-805.

Zhou, X., Wan, X., Mu, B., Du, D. and Spence, C., 2015. Crossmodal associations and subjective ratings of Asian noodles and the impact of the receptacle. Food Quality and Preference 41: 141-150.

4. The sense of sound

R. Haas

Institute of Marketing & Innovation, University of Natural Resources and Life Sciences Vienna (Universität für Bodenkultur Wien), Feistmantelstr. 4, 1180 Vienna, Austria; rainer.haas@boku.ac.at

Abstract

Sound is definitely not the first thing, which comes into the mind of most scientists or practitioners when they think about creating new food products or new restaurant meals. But an increasing number of research studies and marketing cases demonstrates that we almost never experience taste in isolation, taste is the result of a 'multisensory flavour perception'. All of our senses are involved in creating a unique taste perception. In this chapter authors give an overview of the state of the art of research about how sound and music influences food shopping and food consumption behaviour. Authors highlight latest research findings about the influence of sound on taste perception and set it into the context of existing marketing theories about heuristics, consumers apply when tasting or evaluating food products. Auditory inputs either received from atmospherics, from opening a package/bottle, from cooking preparations, from sonic seasoning, from the 'soundscape' of the environment in which consumers eat, or simply the sound from chewing our food influences our food product evaluations and flavour perceptions. Successful retail outlets or restaurants enhance the consumption experience by carefully creating the right soundscape. Innovative food companies actively include auditory stimuli either prior or during food and beverage consumption into their food design efforts. Sonic seasoning creates new opportunities for innovative food companies to enhance the multisensory flavour perception without having to add artificial ingredients. Especially for an ageing population, with diminishing taste sensitivity, improving the taste of food by increasing its auditory features such as crispness and crunchiness will gain importance in the near future.

Keywords: soundscape, sensation transference, atmospherics, multisensory flavour perception, sonic seasoning

Esther Sendra and Ángel A. Carbonell-Barrachina (eds.) **Sensory and aroma marketing**
DOI 10.3920/978-90-8686-841-4_4, © Wageningen Academic Publishers 2017

4.1 Introduction

> The eye guides humans into the world. The ear guides the world into humans.
>
> (Philosopher Lorenz Oken)

Eating is a sensual experience. Without sensuality there is no hedonic joy. The emergence of sensory marketing somehow reflects the change how marketing science sees humans. In the last century the view prevailed that human beings are rational, information processing, and decision makers aiming at maximising their satisfaction. The theory of planned behaviour is a result of this paradigm. Another school of thought sees humans as beings, who search for aesthetic, hedonic, symbolic fulfilment in their life, also when they consume (Holbrook and Hirschman, 1982). The sense of sound, as the quote from the philosopher Lorenz Oken above says, guides the world into us, similar as scents and even more than taste of food or beverages does. The perception of sound and taste follows an interplay, which sometimes leads to surprising results.

> Sound is undoubtedly the forgotten flavour sense. Most researchers, when they think about flavour, fail to give due consideration to the sound that a food makes when they bite into and chew it. However, what we hear while eating plays an important role in our perception of the textural properties of food, not to mention our overall enjoyment of the multisensory experience of food and drink.
>
> (Spence, 2015)

In this chapter, we will focus on two aspects, which are crucial to better understand how the sense of sound is relevant for food marketing and food consumption behaviour. The first part focuses on how sound influences our buying behaviour and food consumption, and the second part focuses on how sound influences our taste perception.

4.2 The sound of the marketplace

> Atmospherics is the effort to design buying environments to produce specific emotional effects in the buyer that enhance his purchase probability.
>
> (Kotler, 1973)

Theodore Levitt – one of the most influential marketing thinkers – wrote in 1981 a classical and very influential article about tangible and intangible features of products and services (Levitt, 1981). His focus was on how to make the quality of services visible. The significant contribution of his article is, that it made marketing scholars aware that there is the tangible product – a book, a shaving cream, or a bottle of wine – but there are also intangible parts like warranties, status conveyed by possessing the product or images evoked through advertising. And many others of intangible 'product parts' we encounter at the place of shopping. 'Everybody sells intangibles in the marketplace, no matter what is produced in the factory' (Levitt, 1981). There is the layout of the store, the intensity and colour spectre of the lighting, the temperature, maybe the smell of fresh baked bread or cinnamon reminding us on Christmas times. There is the 'soundscape', maybe it is noisy, a baby crying in the nearby alley, maybe some chilled ambient music is playing in the background. Whatever it is, it will influence on a subliminal level the amount of time we are going to spend in the store. The longer we stay, the higher the probability that we spend more money than we originally intended to.

> The tangible product – a pair of shoes, a refrigerator, a haircut, or a meal – is only a small part of the total consumption package. Buyers respond to the total product. ... One of the most significant features of the total product is the place where it is bought or consumed. In some cases, the place, more specifically the atmosphere of the place, is more influential than the product itself in the purchase decision. In some cases, the atmosphere is the primary product.
>
> (Kotler, 1973)

By using the term 'total product' Kotler (1973) talks in fact about the holistic experience of shopping and consuming food, which goes way beyond our visual senses, it encompasses our tactile sense, hearing, smelling and tasting. In his article he further recommended that marketers should actively include the 'atmospherics' in their marketing efforts: 'atmospherics is the effort to design buying environments to produce specific emotional effects in the buyer that enhance his purchase probability' (Kotler, 1973). So atmospherics could be seen as a very mundane approach to create more sales. But from a poetic of view – which does not have to be necessarily a contradiction to marketing efforts – it could be seen as an effort to positively enhance the experience of consuming and buying food in a *sensual way*. It is not so long ago, maybe 50 to 30 years ago, that fresh markets were common all over European and US cities. Before hygienic standards and regulations forced markets to become overwhelmingly sterile, fresh markets offered a variety of sensual stimuli, which made the shopping experience sensual and unique at least. Alone the smell of fresh fruits and vegetables, the enticing scent of fresh baked bread and rolls intermingling with the smell of fresh caught fish, or meat just getting cut, the colour of blood streams flowing between the butcher stands, the voices of sutlers appraising their produce, none of it orchestrated, nevertheless it provided a holistic shopping experience for all senses.

Whatever view you prefer, the mundane marketing view or the uplifting poetic view, atmospherics is about creating emotions, and music is one of the best means to create emotions. Like scents, music has also the ability to bring memories back to surface. So it is not surprising that scientists put a lot of effort into understanding how music influences our shopping behaviour. One of the first behavioural studies looked at the impact of slow paced and fast paced instrumental background music on shopping behaviour in a supermarket (Milliman, 1982). Not surprisingly it was observed that slow paced background music resulted in a slower flow of customers through the store, and the more time the customers spent in the store, the more money they spent. In fact the difference between fast paced and slow paced music resulted in astounding 38% more sales per day (Milliman, 1982). In a subsequent study 30 years later, it was discovered that not the tempo of the music *per se* is decisive, the slow tempo has to be combined with the right musical mode. Slow paced music only increased sales when played in a minor mode, played in the mayor mode it had no effect on sales (Knoferle *et al.*, 2012). Of course the influence goes beyond the simple difference of tempo and musical mode. It makes a difference if we are familiar with a variety of music styles, and what our preferences are; or if classical music or popular music is played. Areni and Kim (1993) observed that more expensive wine is bought in a wine store when classical music is played compared to a Top 40 music list.

An extensive meta-analysis of studies about the influence of background music in a retail setting analysed 150 scientific papers, the publication years spanning from 1966 to 2006. The analysed studies covered a range of dependent variables, spanning from financial, to attitudinal, to behavioural and emotional factors (Garlin and Owen, 2006) (Table 4.1).

The consistency of the results in the analysed studies implied positive financial returns for background music in a retail context. Summarized the studies identified the following relationships (Garlin and Owen, 2006):
▸ Familiarity with music has a positive effect on the customers and the felt pleasure.
▸ Familiar music with a slower tempo and lower volume increases the time spent in the store and results in higher sales.
▸ Unfamiliar, disliked, loud and fast music shortens shopping time and reduces sales.

Based on these collective findings suitable background music has the ability to influence positively '... affective, attitudinal/perceptual, temporal and behavioural variables. A considerable body of work presents evidence for these effects to provide returns to business in the form of sales value and volume, repeat purchase, rate of spend, quantity purchased and gross margin. Many indirect returns to business are apparent, such as positive perceptions of quality and venue/store brand image' (Garlin and Owen, 2006, 762).

Table 4.1. Dependent variables studied in background music (adapted from Garlin and Owen, 2006).

Variable category	% studies (n=150)	Variations or descriptors
Affective	41	mood, arousal, pleasure, emotion, nostalgia
Financial returns	25	value of sales, repeat purchase, items purchased, rate of spend, quantity purchased, gross margin
Attitudinal/perceptual	24	liking, brand loyalty, product evaluation, quality perceptions, experience satisfaction, perception of visual stimuli, service quality perceptions, price sensitivity, expectations, intentions, social identification, status perception
Temporal effects	20	duration perceived/actual, service time, unplanned time, time to serve customers, time to decision-make, time to consume, duration of music listening
Behavioural	10	patronage frequency, store choice, behaviour speed, affiliation, items examined/handled, in-store traffic flow, impulse behaviour, recommend service, number of customers leaving before served

As much as music can have a positive effect on our shopping behaviour and food consumption; noise can have a negative impact. In an experiment, noise was used to put respondents under stress. Then, they were asked to rate the pleasure they received from different sweet solutions. The higher the noise, the more the respondents preferred sweeter solutions (Ferber and Cabanac, 1987), which sheds an interesting light on the influence of stress and sugar consumption. Talking about higher sugar consumption, it should be remarked as a side note that temperature, another atmospheric variable, in supermarkets, homes or offices with air condition could play a role in promoting obesity. Consumption of energy dense food increases during prolonged times of cold temperature (Keith *et al.*, 2006), so imagine a society where people spend a lot of the time in rooms cooler than necessary and connect it with calorie intake.

Next to supermarkets, restaurants are important food marketplaces, where music plays a role in modulating the food consumption experience. Research found patrons tend to drink more and eat more, when they enjoy the music being played in a restaurant (Milliman, 1986). Ambient and pleasant perceived music promotes slower eating, longer time spans of meals and an increased consumption of food and beverages (Caldwell and Hibbert, 2002). On contrary in restaurants with loud, fast or disturbing music, patrons have the tendency to spend less time (North and Hargreaves, 1996).

One of the pioneering restaurants in this field is the Fat Duck restaurant from Heston Blumenthal. He serves a signature dish called 'Sound of the sea'. It is seafood paired with a conch shell containing headphones. People can listen to the sound of the ocean while eating seafood. Research showed that people perceive seafood as tasting significantly better and not salty anymore while listening to the sounds of the ocean compared to other soundtracks (Spence, 2016, pp. 98). The 'synaestethic' matching of sound and taste became a new and fascinating research field (Spence, 2013). Together with the Fat Duck restaurant, Charles Spence and his team from the Crossmodal Research Laboratory at Oxford University discovered that you actually can enhance the bitterness in a bittersweet toffee by playing a low pitched sound. If you play for the same bittersweet toffee a higher pitched sound, it enhances the sweetness perception (Spence, 2013).

In Brussels local chocolatiers, scientists and musicians started the 'Sound of Chocolate' project, where they paired specific pieces of music with different kinds of chocolate (Blondeel, 2017). Chocolatiers developed for this project new chocolate pralines, which are sold in boxes containing a music CD with songs especially designed to enhance the tasting experience while listening to the music.

The pairing of flavours with music pieces followed a two-step process. First, they paired the identity of the chocolatier with a local music band to make sure the music was in the mind of the chocolatier, when creating his formula. Second, they tested the songs to better understand how they can improve the sweetness, creaminess or bitterness of the chocolate. By collecting taste ratings of consumers of tasting the same chocolate while listening to music pieces, which were designed to increase sweetness/creaminess or bitterness/roughness perception, Carvalho et al. (2017) found that the songs had the expected effect. Soft smooth sounds consisting of long-consonant-legato notes corresponded with higher ratings of sweetness and creaminess. Sounds consisting of short-dissonant-staccato notes corresponded with perceiving chocolate as more bitter and rougher (Carvalho et al., 2017).

Another innovative example of using sound to improve the dining experience is an in-flight playlist of 13 songs offered by British Airways to its travellers. The songs on the playlist were specifically chosen to improve the taste of the dishes offered during flights (Spence, 2015).

4.3 The sound of taste

> There is darkness, there is light, there are men and women. There is food. There
> are restaurants, disease; there is work, traffic, ... The days as we know them, the
> world as we imagine the world. ... First, overwhelmed with grief ... and then
> no sense of smell ... that is the disease. They call it severe olfactory syndrome.
> ... Life goes on. The food becomes spicier, saltier, more sweet, more sour, you
> get used to it.
>
> (Quote from the movie 'Perfect Sense')

In the movie called 'Perfect Sense' with Ian McGregor and Eva Green, the story plays in
a fictitious future world, where an unknown worldwide disease takes away one of the five
senses after the other with every new outbreak. First, the sense of smell disappeared and
people discovered that they do not taste as much of their food as they did before. To cope
with this challenge, the hero (Ian McGregor), who is a chef in a famous restaurant, uses more
spices and salt. After that the people lost their taste sense, he starts to change the texture and
structure of his meals to compensate the loss of taste perception with an auditory experience.

In a similar way as scents improve the intensity of flavours, or trigger memories in our brain,
the experience of eating and enjoying food is influenced by sound. Texture and structure
release sensory stimulants while chewing, resulting also in an auditory experience, which tells
our brain something about the quality of the food we consume. On a theoretical level, the
phenomenon that one sensory perception influences the quality of another sensory stimulus
is called sensation transference (Cheskin, 1972), multisensory flavour perception (Spence,
2013) or crossmodal modulation of taste by sound (Carvalho *et al.*, 2016).

Before we talk more about crossmodal modulation of taste by sound, it is necessary to
remind us that in general our perception is biased. It is not only selective – which means
we suppress information, which contradicts our opinions and search for information which
confirms our world view to achieve cognitive balance – but we are also prone to use one
single attribute of an object for an overall evaluation of this object. The theoretical marketing
terms, which are related to these phenomena and which need to be explained shortly are
called 'halo effect', 'sensation transference' and 'quality cues'.

The halo effect is defined as the 'tendency in rating to be influenced by general impression
or attitude when trying to judge separate traits' (English, 1934). The halo effect goes back to
the psychologist Edward Thorndike and a paper, which he published in 1920 in the *Journal
of Applied Psychology* with the title 'a constant error in psychological ratings' (Thorndike,
1920). He discovered in two studies, one about managers rating their employees of two large

companies in respect to traits such as reliability, intelligence, technical skills, ... and one of officers evaluating military pilots, that once the superiors had a general positive impression of a person, they tended to evaluate all single traits as equally positive. For example, a positive physical appearance (bearing, neatness, voice, energy, and endurance) resulted in a positive evaluation of intelligence and technical skills. Only few people were rated good in one trait and bad in other traits. Later studies found that the first impression of a person has a strong impact how we evaluate them consecutively. In this respect the saying 'you only get one chance to make a first impression', reflects the scientific knowledge of how we tend to evaluate people. Even in studies where people get enough information to apply independent assessment of attributes they 'halo' intensely and believe that the overall rating is the result of their individual judgements of specific attributes, but in fact it is the other way round (Nisbett and Wilson, 1977).

A marketing application of the halo effect is the use of celebrities as testimonials in advertising campaigns. Once a celebrity is seen as trustworthy or admired for its beauty, their positive image is the halo, which sets any product, they promote into a positive light. The same goes for the image of corporations or brands (Leuthesser *et al.*, 1995).

> Much of our thinking about company performance is shaped by the halo effect ... when a company is growing and profitable, we tend to infer that it has a brilliant strategy, a visionary CEO (chief executive officer), motivated people, and a vibrant culture. When performance falters, we are quick to say the strategy was misguided, the CEO became arrogant, the people were complacent, and the culture stodgy ... At first, all of this may seem like harmless journalistic hyperbole, but when researchers gather data that are contaminated by the halo effect – including not only press accounts but interviews with managers – the findings are suspect.
>
> (Rosenzweig, 2007)

Similar to using antecedent auditory or nasal sensations to form a taste experience, our brain seems to use one specific attribute to evaluate people, brands, food products to name a few. As if one attributes 'shines' over all the other attributes and colours them in a specific meaning. This phenomenon has many important implications for marketing and food design and is even expressed in different theories. In *Gestalt* theory (*Gestalt* is a German word and means 'shape', 'form') it is said that 'the whole is other than the sum of the parts', which means that it is difficult or sometimes even impossible to isolate the impact of single product attributes on the perception of its *Gestalt* (Dewey, 2007). Think at a chess game, to better understand *Gestalt* theory. The presence of each chess piece influences the meaning of all other existing chess pieces. Move one piece and it changes the *Gestalt* of the chess game, despite the fact, that still the same number of chess pieces are on the board.

When the aesthetics or packaging of a product influences the perception of its intrinsic qualities such as taste or freshness, this is what Cheskin (1972) referred to as sensation transference. He observed that consumers transfer their feelings about packaging or design features towards the whole product itself. Cheskin (1972) recommended changing the colour of a specific margarine brand from white to yellow and the packaging from paper to foil. Consumers afterwards perceived the taste and quality of the same margarine as better and sales increased. Other examples of sensation transference are when consumers estimate the cooling capacity of a refrigerator higher when the inside colour of the refrigerator is more blue. Or they say a skin cream smells differently when only the colour of the skin cream got changed.

The above-mentioned 'sound of chocolate'-project is a practical application of sensation transference. What works with chocolate also works with beer: '... soundtracks that had been specifically developed to evoke a specific taste can effectively be used in order to influence the participants' beer tasting experience' (Carvalho *et al.*, 2016). Identical beer got different ratings of sweetness, bitterness, sourness, and alcohol content dependent on what kind of soundtrack the participants listened to. For example, when respondent listened to the sourness soundtrack, the tasted beer was not only perceived as more sour but also with higher alcohol content (Carvalho *et al.*, 2016). North (2012) discovered that playing specific songs promotes the perception of 'zingy' and 'refreshing' notes in wine, while other songs made the taste perception of the wine 'more powerful and heavier'. When music or sounds change the perception of flavours this sensation transference is called 'sonic seasoning' (Spence, 2016). Why specific sounds enhance specific flavours is still an unresolved issue. Some argue that it is the result of a halo effect. Depending on what people think or feel when listening to a specific song, and how much they like the song, this positive or negative evaluation becomes the halo, which 'shines' into the taste perception (Spence, 2016).

It can be assumed that sonic seasoning works with many different kinds of food products besides chocolate, wine, and beer. Also food consumption situations in restaurants, as the examples of British Airways or the Fat Duck restaurant with their signature seafood dish with ocean sounds show, can be enhanced by applying crossmodal modulation of taste. And sonic seasoning not only works with music but also with extrinsic product sounds, which are related to the food product being consumed. Examples are the sound being made in a kitchen, the simmering of a pot of soup, the hammering sounds of knives on a wood board cutting vegetables, the sizzling and mouth-watering sound of a steak being fried. Knoferle *et al.* (2011) made an experiment where he exposed consumers to the sound of a coffee machine prior to coffee tasting. They found that the perceived taste of the coffee was rated better after listening to the sound of the coffee machine. In a subsequent study, they observed that this effect was only valid for consumers who highly enjoy product sounds.

Similar to the halo effect is the theory about quality cues. When consumers evaluate a product they often use quality cues, which is a specific kind of information. Why they use specific information or attributes to interfere quality is still a not sufficiently understood process. Examples of such interferences are colour and fat content as indicators for better taste and tenderness of meat, or animal welfare as an indicator for healthier food products (Grunert, 2005), or regional/local food production as a quality cue to fresher and tastier food (Cerjak *et al.*, 2014). Consumers also use organic as a quality cue for healthier food, simply because it is organic, even if scientific studies yet did not find evidence to support this assumption (Dangour *et al.*, 2009).

Especially for low involvement products – and in most buying situations, food can be considered to be a low involvement product – consumers often use one information as quality cue to form a judgement about other attributes as freshness, taste or healthiness of the food product (Wansink, 2003). Under uncertainty or difficult situations to evaluate quality, the usage of extrinsic quality cues like 'brand name' increases (Verbeke and Ward, 2006). In an experiment where consumers had to evaluate the taste of different beer brands, some consumers refused to taste specific beers because they were familiar with the brand. They obviously used the quality cue 'brand name' to judge the taste of the beer (Cerjak *et al.*, 2010).

These psychological phenomena make us aware, that the joy of food is a multi-sensual experience, which reaches beyond the sweet, sour, salty, bitter, and umami taste receptors on our tongue. Using other sensory stimulants as smell and sound can interfere with the perception of taste. Crispness and crunchiness are desirable quality attributes to enjoy food. But they are also '… very complex concepts, which combine a wide range of perceptions, such as sounds, fracture characteristics, density and geometry' (Fillion and Kilcast, 2002). Many innovative food companies engage for that reason in sound design. Bahlsen, the German cookie company, works with a team of cookie testers who carry special microphones in their ears to record the sound of crunchiness. Afterwards recipes are adjusted to achieve the right crunch. Bahlsen even develops different sounds of crunchiness for different target groups. For young people they bake cookies emanating a strong crisp exciting sound, for older people the bake cookies with a softer, less noisy, crunch and bite (Kotler and Keller, 2009).

Multi-national food corporations such as Nestlé, Unilever, Procter & Gamble or Kellogg's invest in research to improve the auditory sensation of their leading brands. Nestlé uses a

'Crustimeter' to measure the acoustic sensations during breaking or chewing of food (Czaja, 2005). One of the success factors of Unilever's Magnum ice cream is the distinctive cracking sound when consumers bite into the hard chocolate shell to dive with their teeth into the sweet softness of the ice cream. For a short time Unilever changed the recipe of Magnum and the distinctive sound of cracking chocolate bits got lost and resulted in immediate consumer complaints (Spence, 2016, pp. 89). Also Kellogg's understands that the crunchiness of their cereals is of crucial importance for the pleasure consumers derive of it. Not only because of the texture but also because of the sound it makes during mastication. It is not surprising that crunchiness is vital for the success of potato chips and it influences our taste perception. If you manipulate the crunching sound of potato chips, while being chewed, you can increase their perceived freshness by 15% (Zampini and Spence, 2004).

Sound design is applied in many industries, the car industry was one of the first who started to look for specific sounds of engines or more important the sound of a slammed car door, which is an excellent example of combining audio with the touch and feel of a product. Research showed that consumers infer the quality and solidity of the car from the feel and sound of slamming its door. But it is not only the sound of slammed car doors, teams of audio specialists work on. BMW employs its Active Sound Design for the M5 to generate fake engine noise of the bi-turbocharged V-8 engine inside the car over its stereo speakers. According to BMW '... the Active Sound Design control unit ensures an even spread of sound across all five seats of the new BMW M5, while observing the legal guidelines governing noise emissions inside and outside the car' (Goodwin, 2011). Depending on the kind of car different sound design objectives are pursued. General Motors or Honda use for their luxury cars Active Noise Cancellation technology to cancel out engine and cabin noise. Active Noise Cancellation superimposes one audio wave in an exact 180-degree angle on another audio wave thus cancelling out the noise. On the other side, Toyota uses external speakers on its car model 'Prius' to make pedestrians aware of the silently approaching hybrid car.

In the food industry, food designers work often on the haptics, the touch of food products, combined with auditory sensations. Specifically designed beer bottles play with those haptics to evoke a subliminal touch while holding your beer bottle standing at a party. What those bottles have in common are upraised portions of glass, which, allow beer drinkers to slowly wander with their fingers over the uneven surface, generating a nice subliminal touch. There is even a built-in 'fiddle factor' on beer bottles, because beer drinkers love to fiddle with their nails under the label to tear it off (Horn, 2013).

What the slamming of the car door is for car drivers is the opening of a beer bottle for beer drinkers. In the past, old beer bottles opened with a 'plopp' due to the way in which the cap was pulled off. Nowadays beer bottles open with a 'ziiisch'. Ottakringer, an Austrian beer company, developed a special beer cap to achieve the formerly well known 'plopp', because their market research has shown that beer, which opens with a 'plopp'-sound is perceived to be fresher (Czaja, 2005). Other internationally better-known examples of 'sonic differentiation' are the 'Snapple Pop' or the swing-top beer bottle used by beer companies such as the Dutch brand Grolsch (Spence and Wang, 2015), the Austrian Kapsreiter Landbier, The German Tettnanger or the French Fischer brewery. Sonic differentiation aims at differentiating a food product from competitors by the opening sound. Snapple argues that the 'Snapple Pop' also signals to consumers that the product is fresh and has not been tampered with (Spence and Wang, 2015).

4.4 Conclusions

Summarizing it is crucial to understand that we almost never experience taste in isolation. There is a constantly growing body of research emphasizing that taste is the result of a 'multisensory flavour perception' (Spence, 2013). The flavours we experience are the outcome of the combination of auditory inputs, the receiving taste buds on our tongue, olfactory perception of food and beverage scents and trigeminal stimuli. For example 80% of our 'taste' perception stems from olfactory receptors in our nose (Spence, 2013). Auditory inputs either received from the atmospherics, from opening the package/bottle, from cooking preparations, from sonic seasoning, from the 'soundscape' of the environment in which we eat, or from chewing the food influence our flavour perceptions. There are restaurants on the market, which serve meals to their patrons with sonic seasoning or airlines providing soundtracks to improve the holistic experience of eating. Sonic seasoning offers new opportunities for product development to create food products, which could enhance the eating or drinking experience without having to add artificial ingredients. In respect to the demographic trend of an ageing population, with diminishing taste sensitivity, improving the taste of food by increasing its crispness and crunchiness will gain importance in the near future. Grocery stores, supermarket outlets, restaurants, all should consciously design the available atmospherics to improve the shopping experience. Food marketers and food scientists working in retail, gastronomy or food design are well advised to use the growing body of research about multi-sensory flavour perception to create new joyful sensual experiences for food and beverage consumers.

References

Areni, C.S. and Kim, D., 1993. The influence of background music on shopping behavior: classical versus top-40 music in wine store. Advances in Consumer Research 20: 336-340.

Blondeel, F., 2017. The sound of chocolate. Available at: http://www.thesoundofchocolate.be.

Caldwell, C. and Hibbert, S.A., 2002. The influence of music tempo and musical preference on restaurant patrons' behavior. Psychology and Marketing 19: 895-917.

Carvalho, F.R., Wang, Q.J., Van Ee, R., Persoone, D. and Spence, C., 2017. 'Smooth operator': music modulates the perceived creaminess, sweetness, and bitterness of chocolate. Appetite 108: 383-390.

Carvalho, F.R., Wang, Q.J., Van Ee, R. and Spence, C., 2016. The influence of soundscapes on the perception and evaluation of beers. Food Quality and Preference 52: 32-41.

Cerjak, M., Haas, R., Brunner, F. and Tomić, M., 2014. What motivates consumers to buy traditional food products? Evidence from Croatia and Austria using word association and laddering interviews. British Food Journal 116: 1726-1747.

Cerjak, M., Haas, R. and Kovacic, D., 2010. Brand familiarity and tasting in conjoint analysis: an experimental study with Croatian beer consumers. British Food Journal 112: 561-579.

Cheskin, L., 1972. Marketing success. How to achieve it. Cahners Books, Boston, MA, USA, 64.

Czaja, W., 2005. Food-design: mit Ziegel und Lenden. Die Presse. Available at: http://tinyurl.com/kcxxbqa.

Dangour, A.D., Dodhia, S.K., Hayter, A., Allen, E., Lock, K. and Uauy, R., 2009. Nutritional quality of organic foods: a systematic review. American Journal of Clinical Nutrition 90(3): 680-685.

Dewey, R., 2007. The whole is other than the sum of the parts. Available at: http://tinyurl.com/nywlyje.

English, H.B., 1934. A student's dictionary of psychological terms. Harper and Brothers Publisher, New York, NY, USA, pp. 131.

Ferber, C. and Cabanac, M., 1987. Influence of noise on gustatory affective ratings and preference for sweet or salt. Appetite 8: 229-235.

Fillion, L. and Kilcast, D., 2002. Consumer perception of crispness and crunchiness in fruits and vegetables. Food Quality and Preference 13: 23-29.

Garlin, F.V. and Owen, K., 2006. Setting the tone with the tune: a meta-analytic review of the effects of background music in retail settings. Journal of Business Research 59: 755-764.

Goodwin, A., 2011. BMW M5 generates fake engine noise using stereo. Available at: http://tinyurl.com/mdmxjw3.

Grunert, K.G., 2005. Food quality and safety: consumer perception and demand. European Review of Agricultural Economics 32: 369-391.

Holbrook, M.B. and Hirschman, E.C., 1982. The experiential aspects of consumption: consumer fantasies, feelings, and fun. Journal of Consumer Research 9: 132-140.

Horn, L., 2013. Why so many beer bottles suddenly look so different. Available at: http://tinyurl.com/brj8c2g.

Keith, S.W., Redden, D.T., Katzmarzyk, P.T., Boggiano, M.M., Hanlon, E.C., Benca, R.M., Ruden, D., Pietrobelli, A., Barger, J.L., Fontaine, K.R., Wang, C., Aronne, L.J., Wright, S.M., Baskin, M., Dhurandhar, N.V, Lijoi, M.C., Grilo, C.M., DeLuca, M., Westfall, A.O. and Allison, D.B., 2006. Putative contributors to the secular increase in obesity: exploring the roads less traveled. International Journal of Obesity 30: 1585-1594.

Knoferle, K.M., Spangenberg, E.R., Herrmann, A. and Landwehr, J.R., 2012. It is all in the mix: the interactive effect of music tempo and mode on in-store sales. Marketing Letters 23: 325-337.

Knoferle, K.M., Sprott, D.E., Landwehr, J.R. and Hermann, A., 2011. It's the sizzle that sells: crossmodal influences of acoustic product cues varying in auditory pleasantness on taste perceptions. PhD-thesis, University of St. Gallen, 91 pp. Available at: http://tinyurl.com/kdgxmua.

Kotler, P., 1973. Atmospherics as a marketing tool. Journal of Retailing: 48-65.

Kotler, P. and Keller, K.L., 2009. Marketing management. Pearson Prentice Hall, Upper Saddle River, NJ, USA, 816 pp.

Leuthesser, L., Kohli, C.S. and Harich, K.R., 1995. Brand equity: the halo effect measure. European Journal of Marketing 29: 57-66.

Levitt, T., 1981. Marketing intangible products and product intangibles. Harvard Business Review. Available at: http://tinyurl.com/mzll74z.

Milliman, R., 1982. Using background music to affect the behavior of supermarket shoppers. Journal of Marketing 46: 86-91.

Milliman, R.E., 1986. The influence of background music on the behavior of restaurant patrons. Israel Annals of Psychiatry and Related Disciplines 13: 286-289.

Nisbett, R.E. and Wilson, T.D., 1977. The halo effect: evidence for unconscious alteration of judgments. Journal of Personality and Social Psychology 35: 250-256.

North, A.C., 2012. The effect of background music on the taste of wine. British Journal of Psychology 103: 293-301.

North, A.C. and Hargreaves, D.J., 1996. The effects of music on responses to a dining area. Journal of Environmental Psychology 16: 55-64.

Rosenzweig, P.M., 2007. The halo effect ... and the eight other business delusions that deceive managers. Free Press, New York, NY, USA, pp. 256.

Spence, C., 2013. Multisensory flavour perception. Current Biology 23: R365-R369.

Spence, C., 2015. Eating with our ears: assessing the importance of the sounds of consumption on our perception and enjoyment of multisensory flavour experiences. Flavour 4(3).

Spence, C., 2016. Sound: the forgotten flavor sense. Multisensory flavor perception: from fundamental neuroscience through to the marketplace. Elsevier Ltd, New York, NY, USA, pp. 81-105.

Spence, C. and Wang, Q.J., 2015. Sensory expectations elicited by the sounds of opening the packaging and pouring a beverage. Flavour 4(35).

Thorndike, E.L., 1920. A constant error in psychological ratings. Journal of Applied Psychology 4: 25-29.

Verbeke, W. and Ward, R.W., 2006. Consumer interest in information cues denoting quality, traceability and origin: an application of ordered probit models to beef labels. Food Quality and Preference 17: 453-467.

Wansink, B., 2003. Response to 'Measuring consumer response to food products'. Sensory tests that predict consumer acceptance. Food Quality and Preference 14: 23-26.

Zampini, M. and Spence, C., 2004. The role of auditory cues in modulating the perceived crispness and staleness of potato chips. Journal of Sensory Studies 19: 347-363.

5. The sense of taste

J. Rybanská and Ľ. Nagyová

Slovak University of Agriculture, Faculty of Economics and Management, Department of Marketing and Trade, Tr. A. Hlinku 2, 949 76 Nitra, Slovak Republic; jane.rybanska@gmail.com

Abstract

Taste is the most specific sense humans possess. It is very difficult to link food taste with consumers' preference; what might have a great taste for one, the other might not enjoy at all. Taste is closely linked with the smell sense, but it is significantly affected by other senses and sensory stimuli. In this chapter, first it will be explained what the taste is and how a consumer perceives the taste, how taste centres operate in the brain, how does taste relate with other senses and how it can be influenced. The text is also complemented by some interest findings of taste. Secondly, the taste determinants and how taste determines buying behaviour will be explained. It is generally assumed that the taste would be significantly connected to the food quality, but it is not always true. Often, lower quality products are the most delicious, for some consumers. The same rule can be applied to the price and it has its reason. Many worldwide research studies dealing with the taste will be provided.

Keywords: brand, gustatory stimuli, taste centres, taste determinants, product quality

Esther Sendra and Ángel A. Carbonell-Barrachina (eds.) **Sensory and aroma marketing**
DOI 10.3920/978-90-8686-841-4_5, © Wageningen Academic Publishers 2017

5.1 Introduction

Taste is the sense that allows us to perceive the chemicals dissolved in water
or saliva, and it is very closely related to the sense of smell

Research on gustatory system achieved enormous progress over the last decade. Taste, according to the International Organization for Standardization (ISO, 2008), is defined as the complex olfactory, gustatory, and nervous stimulus that is perceived during tasting of substances (Seo and Hummel, 2011). Taste is the sense that allows us to perceive the chemicals dissolved in water or saliva, and it is very closely related to the sense of smell. Smell is actually the most essential sense, and not only from a marketing perspective. For example, if a consumer smells something good (in its opinion), the olfactory receptors in the nose connect directly with the limbic system, which is in control of our emotions and memories that depends on the smell; in this way, if we like the smell, the result is immediate craving for this food. With other sensory perceptions human body reacts and responds to sensory stimuli. But with smell, subconscious reactions come first, and later, the conscious response happens. When the sense of smell is damaged, then, taste is impaired as well; however, even when suffering a strong cold, consumers are able to distinguish between the sweet and salty tastes, for example.

5.2 Physiology of the taste

Consumers can identify all tastes anywhere in the tongue, but the sensitivity
to each taste in each part of the tongue is different

5.2.1 Phantosmia (phantom smell) – When you perceive a flavour that does not exist in food

'The taste is imperceptible by nose or mouth, but by your brain,' says Mark Friedmann, a scientist at the Monell Chemical Senses Centre in Philadelphia, a scientific institute for multidisciplinary research on taste, smell, and chemosensory irritation.

The brain is an extremely complex computational tool, containing about 100 billion neurons, but nevertheless it is possible to convince the brain to 'think' that it perceives a flavour (such as, salty or sweet), even when that ingredient is not included in a specific food at all. This phenomenon is called 'phantom smell'. This name is created by the phenomenon of so-called 'phantom limb' – the people who had amputated limb, have a feeling that it is still part of their bodies, and often experience pain at the amputated limb. Both phantom phenomena do have in common the real feelings related to the non-existing facts.

The research of phantom smells has been linked with specific diet habits of certain populations. The consumption of salt and sugar in foods is growing. In the US, the average American consumed to 3,400 mg of salt per day in 2005 and 2006, while the dose recommended by physicians is 2,300 mg of salt per day. In 2005, the average American consumed amount of sugar, which corresponded to 335 calories, in the group of women 230 calories, while the diet experts advise daily consumption limitations of sugar to 150 calories for men and 100 calories for women.

Based on the undertaken research, the manufacturers decided to reduce the salt and sugar content in foods, but the customers' expectations were not met; and, there are many more examples like this. In 2007, Campbell Soup Company decided to reduce the salt content in their canned soup; however, their sales gradually declined. Therefore, in 2011 the company announced that sodium content per portion will be increased again from 400 mg to 650 mg. In 2004, General Mills came on the market with cereal s with reduced sugar content; however, 3 years later, their sugar-reduced cereals were taken off from the market due to a lack of consumers' interest. According to the Coca-Cola Annual Report, in 2014 the sales of Sprite with reduced sugar content dropped significantly by one third (Horák, 2015).

In the study published by Marion Emorine in May 2015, it is indicated that if a flavour associated with salt (e.g. ham flavour) is added to a meal, consumers will consider this food to be salty, although it had no added salt, because there was a scent that evokes salinity (Horák, 2015).

5.2.2 Physiology

Taste stimulus is the substance dissolved in saliva. Threshold values for basic tastes are very low; our tongue can recognize the sweetness of one teaspoon of sugar dissolved in 10 litres of water (Atkinson *et al.*, 2003). Gustatory system consists of taste receptors located on the upper surface of tongue, the relevant parts of the brain and neural pathways. A taste centre is located in the parietal lobe of the cerebral cortex (Figure 5.1), where the combination of basic inputs creates the final taste. The resulting taste is not affected only by the composition of food, but also by its temperature, consistency, appearance, and above all the scent.

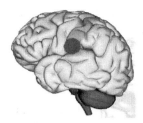

Figure 5.1. The gustatory complex.

Taste receptors of the tongue are present in the taste buds. At the surface of each taste bud, thin hair like extensions sprout and extend over the surface of the tongue, coming in contact with the solution in the mouth; this creates an electrical impulse that travels to the brain (Atkinson *et al.*, 2003). Each taste bud has an onion shaped form and comprises 50 to 100 taste cells. From the morphological point of view, taste buds can be divided into 4 groups (Yamamoto and Ishimaru, 2012):

▸ The first group consists of dark cells.
▸ The second group consists of light cells, responsible for recognition of bitter, sweet, and umami tastes, that are able to release adenosine triphosphate (ATP) at a non-vesicular level.
▸ In the third group, there are transitional cells that mediate the transfer of sour taste and form the neural synapses in the taste buds.
▸ The fourth group consists of round progenitor cells for the previous three groups, within the basal compartment of taste buds.

The perception of the salt taste is influenced by the ion and water homeostasis in the body. In humans, there are taste receptors to distinguish bitter, salty, sweet, sour, and umami tastes. Umami name is derived from Japanese (*umai* = tasty, delicate). The specific taste receptor for umami was discovered at the end of the 20th century and distinguishes the amino acid glutamate (glutamic acid) and its salts (glutamates). The first food with umami taste one usually meets is the breast milk (Ninomiya, 1998). Recent research shows that human body might possess also receptors for recognizing 'other' flavours. Galindo *et al.* (2011) in their research, for example, they talk about 'fat' taste. There are a number of other flavours helping to characterize more accurately flavouring substances in food; these are created when the basic flavours are combined. For example, the fat taste (Laugerette *et al.*, 2007), calcium taste (Tordoff and Sandell, 2009), metallic, astringent, spicy, or *kokumi* taste (Dunkel *et al.*, 2007). Sensitivity to various taste stimuli vary according to the precise place on the tongue. Consumers can identify the different tastes anywhere on the tongue excluding its middle part. However, the greatest sensitivity to the sweet taste is on the tip of the tongue, that to the salty and sour tastes are on the sides, and that to the bitter taste is on the back of the tongue, while the greatest sensitivity to umami is located in the centre of the tongue (Hultén, 2011). A simple taste map is shown on Figure 5.2, where the areas of highest sensitivities are depicted.

However, some researchers believe that it could be otherwise. They assume that taste buds are indeed placed across all the tongue areas, but all of them are able to distinguish all five tastes. The brain is able to distinguish which receptors are stimulated, so consumers feel the different tastes. What is the taste of food and what flavours do we perceive are complex processes (Lawrence, 1998).

Given that the taste is perceived on the tongue and soft palate (Smith and Margolskee, 2001), it can be said that the oral cavity is the place of the final food analysis before its consumption, which in some cases prevents the intake of harmful and toxic substances followed possibly by poisoning and death (Jelen, 2011).

Human begins to recognize tastes just after birth. New-borns prefer sweet food over that with other tastes. A characteristic new-born's response to sweet taste is a relaxed expression, sometimes suggesting a smile. It is believed that this is because the breast milk has a sweet taste. New-born responses to sour taste are pursed lips or nose wrinkling (Atkinson *et al.*, 2003). For children aged around 2 years, there is a change of perception of bitter and sweet tastes, with girls being better in distinguishing between sour and sweet tastes. The best sensitivity receptors, in particular to the sweet taste, are those of children aged 8-14 years (Daly *et al.*, 2012).

Several studies have shown that the sense of taste changes with the age. One of the first tested differences is that sensitivity to taste stimulus decreases with ageing (Methven *et al.*, 2012). In this way, the older consumers are, the lower is their taste sensitivity, and the higher are

Figure 5.2. Traditional taste map.

the thresholds needed to perceive or identify the different tastes. Mojet *et al.* (2003) found that with higher age, the person needs comparatively higher concentration to distinguish the particular tastes than when young. It is estimated that up to one third of elderly people suffer from insufficient or disappeared taste stimuli. In addition to age, change in taste sensations is caused by other factors that are associated with aging taste buds. The most affected is the bitter taste, followed by sour, salty and sweet at the end (Kaneda *et al.,* 2000). These are the reasons why some old people often say that food was tastier when they were young; it was not the food what was tastier, but their senses which were better.

Taste is a very specific sense and although initially can be subjective after proper training of the subjects, this subjectivity can be eliminated. Nowadays, sensory analysis of foods can be carried out, and taste sensitivity can be evaluated using food where the ingredients and concentrations are known, and using solutions with different concentrations of substances (Landis *et al.,* 2009). Sensory analysis is now a significantly advancing trend, which plays an important role in food testing. It is known that the perception of flavour and aroma of (not just) food is a dynamic phenomenon (Lawless and Heymann, 2010). Food companies around the world in recent years are greatly interested in the use of sensory analysis of foods to try to meet consumers' needs and demands. There is no universal preference for food taste, so, sensory analysis should be carried out among the targeted consumers. Sensory analysis of foods and other tasting tests are used in marketing studies to evaluate their influence on consumers' behaviour.

Taste stimuli are often associated with other sensory stimuli, especially visual and olfactory. Sight plays a significant role in taste perception. Taste of the colourless and formless food is extremely difficult to recognize. Consumers need visual tips (information) to be able to identify the flavours and tastes correctly (Lawrence, 1998). There is currently only a small amount of research dedicated to the taste and its effect of consumer preference, because the topic is very diverse and highly subjective. Mirmiran *et al.* (2010) found that the most attractive foods for consumers are high-calorie and fat foods, and that they affect the human brain in a similar way to the action of cocaine or heroin: both activate dopamine release. Thus and in this way, addiction to high-calorie junk food can be compared with drug addiction. Mirmiran *et al.* (2010) also found that the effects of addiction to unhealthy diet last about 7 times longer than the consequences of addiction to cocaine or heroin. Lindstrom (2011) agrees with Mirmiran *et al.* (2010) observations, and claimed that foods, such as chocolate, cheese, pasties, hamburgers, fries, etc., belong to most habit forming foods in the world, and their addictiveness is lagging behind perhaps only after alcohol and cigarettes. Lindstrom (2011) also considered salt, monosodium glutamate, sugar, certain sweeteners, colouring agents, caffeine and menthol as highly addictive substances. Foods containing any of these mentioned ingredients were evaluated more positively by consumers, mainly because these substances affect and often improve the taste of the products. Many foodstuffs selling companies are adjusting their recipes to contain sugar, corn syrup, and sodium glutamate to increase their liking among the consumers.

5.2.3 Mother´s food choices during pregnancy influence what child likes to eat after birth

Many years of research have shown that children like the flavour that faced in the first months of life. However, the researchers claim that children may also be affected by mothers' food choices during prenatal period. A study by French scientists have shown that new-borns can recognize aromas they have been exposed to during the final days of gestation. It suggested that a mother's dietary choices could alter the way their baby's sensory system develops and influence their taste before they are even born (Collins, 2012).

'During pregnancy, the uterus is relatively permeable and some portion of the mother's food is headed to the foetus just at that time when the brain is formed. It is likely to have long-term consequences,' said Benoist Schaal from The University of Burgundy in Dijon, who examined the impact of various flavourings on the foetus in the uterus and children in the first months of life (Collins, 2012).

Researchers from the European Centre for Taste Science in Dijon tested 24 babies, half of whose mothers had eaten biscuits laced with aniseed in the ten days leading up to birth. Experiments carried out hours after birth and again four days later showed that the infants whose mothers had eaten the biscuits could recognize, and appeared to enjoy, the smell of aniseed (Collins, 2012).

5.3 Taste determinants and how taste determines buying behaviour

> Taste research is not getting enough attention in sensory marketing; thus, there is a big opportunity in this field

As previously discussed, taste preferences and perception might be very subjective. It is known that each person distinguishes several flavours; however, the consumer preference is not affected only by the product composition, but also by many other factors. The consumer preference is affected by all the factors that are influencing consumer behaviour, such as cultural, social, personal, psychological, and situational factors. For each culture, there are specific traditional dishes related not only to their history, but also to the area where the community exists; examples of these country-specific products are the sheep cheese dumplings in Slovakia, and sushi in Japan. Of course, sushi is also popular in Slovakia and other countries, but certainly not as much as in Japan.

Ongoing globalization is gradually causing the mixing of cultures and so many people have the opportunity to taste and enjoy a variety of dishes. However, it is true that the most popular dishes for everyone are the ones that we grew up on and the taste of these foods is also influencing the perception of others, often non-traditional flavours.

Sense of taste is affected by all factors influencing consumer behaviour, such as the culture that affects our social environment, in particular family and institutions, as well as other groups to which we belong or wish to be part of. During childhood, consumers perceive what their parents, siblings, and friends are eating, and often they like the same food as they do. Man learns by imitating the behaviour of others, and this applies also to the eating habits. Personality factors play a role in the perception of taste, especially in the later stages of our lives, when we start to recognize our own personality and develop ourselves. The psychological factors are among the factors that influence taste perception the most, and include other factors, such as environmental influences, conscious and subconscious influences, but especially marketing, general promotion (not only) of food products, their appearance, shape, packaging, structure, and how do they feel on touch. Situational factors include the particular situations in which a person selects various products. It is known that a hungry man buys more food than a satiated one, and similarly, a hungry person senses food taste differently than when full.

Many researchers have devoted decades to taste research, and there are many different approaches. From a marketing perspective, the research is mainly about testing product samples directly in stores, then research of changes in taste after changes in the product composition, taste in connection with branding, taste investigation in connection with the packaging, and consumer preferences. Selecting the correct method for taste research is extremely important for sellers from a marketing point of view.

The perception of a particular taste is impacted by all other senses. Identifying the taste of colourless and odourless food, that we could not even touch, would be an almost impossible task. The rest of the senses, in combination with other factors, considerably alter not only the perception of the taste but also the taste preferences. As mentioned above, taste research is inextricably linked with smell, because these two senses are very difficult to separate. Molecules of flavour are entering the nasal cavity together with air, where millions of receptors help to carry the information to the brain. Chewing food helps to release more aromas from the mouth to the back of the nose, so close to the olfactory centres where the information is further processed.

The sight is incredibly important for the sense of taste. In order to identify the taste of food, consumers need also the visual information. The better the food looks, the tastier it is expected to be; of course, this may not be true. However, from a marketing point of view, this link between sight (appearance) and taste is extremely important, and it is used many times to sell food taste through the food appearance. The human brain interprets the signals of the taste, smell, vision, and other senses even before they are converted to the sensory experience of tasting food; this could be, among other reasons, why the taste of the same food is perceived in different ways by different consumers.

Velasco *et al.* (2016) reviewed crossmodal correspondences between taste and shape, and their implications for product packaging. They described how customers linked simple flavours, or words describing the simple tastes with a specific shape of product packaging. Based on the various studies, it is known that consumers associated the certain expectations of taste with the logo and the brand. Velasco *et al.* (2016) wrote that there were also fundamental consistencies, which work well also for unknown impulses. The research specifically shows that shape attributes (i.e. straight vs curved, symmetrical vs asymmetrical) affected the taste that is perceived by consumers. The data suggested that people associated certain shape dimensions with flavours based on regular affective significance.

Connection between taste and the rest of the senses has also been studied by Lindstrom (2011). This author found that consumers are fed up with visual cues and gradually become resistant. It is, therefore, necessary to use other senses, including taste, in marketing strategies to a greater degree. He clarified how much the colour of food itself contributes to the sense of taste, to estimate how the product will taste and the expected perception of food quality.

Lindstrom (2011) described and developed studies on the relation among taste and smell with the other senses. Many companies use different scents (smell of coffee in the bakery, the smell of chocolate in a candy store, the smell of French fries in fast food places, etc.) to attract customers, to raise their appetite, but also to influence their perception of food tastes.

Quite often, consumers face the fact that lower quality products (less healthy foods) are the most delicious. This is mainly due to the additives used in those foods; they are often cheaper compared to traditional raw materials but have significant effect on the taste of food. However, many people, even today, prefer to prepare their meal at home. Nowadays, when consumers care greatly about their healthy lifestyle, cooking at home is one of the best options, if time is available. If they do not have the time to cook, customers often seek out for small domestic vendors and with traceable food.

However, most of the food is now just purchased in supermarkets. That is one of the main reasons for the use of various additives (Figure 5.3); the main reason to use these chemicals is that such foods are required to last longer and have a longer shelf life. In some products, the need for additives is so great that they are used even in organic foods. Preservatives, dyes, flavourings and sweeteners are the best known and most commonly used additives in contemporary foods (Lawrence, 1998).

In an experiment, subjects had to determine which of the drinks they would choose, even though all 3 tasted exactly the same. The 3 beverages had the same composition, but with different amounts of orange dye. The subjects stated that the intermediate orange product was the preferred one. This experiment confirmed that consumers perceive the taste and the linked preference also with our sight. Beverage in the middle probably looks the most natural and healthy. During the processing of food products, many of them lose their colour and look less attractive and tasty. Therefore, dyes are used to enhance colour attributes; they make food look more beautiful and, thus, more delicious (Lawrence, 1998).

The most commonly used food colouring agents are listed in Table 5.1. Other chemical substances besides the food colourings are also used in processed foods. The best known are flavourings, flavour enhancers, and sweeteners. Foodstuffs may contain over a thousand of chemical compounds, most of them natural ones, that together form the flavour of a particular food. Many of the naturally occurring compounds are very volatile, and therefore cannot be used in long-life products. Instead, substitute additives are used (Lawrence, 1998). One of the most famous flavour enhancers is monosodium glutamate (E621 or MSG), which occurs in virtually all foods containing proteins. It is added to many snacks and other foods. E621 has been used as a food additive for decades. Over the years, the FDA has received many reports of adverse reactions to foods containing E621. These reactions – known as MSG symptom complex – include: headache, flushing, sweating, facial pressure or tightness,

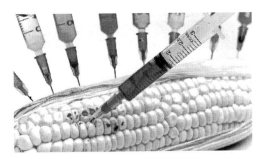

Figure 5.3. Additives are used in many products (http://bembu.com/9-food-additives-to-avoid).

numbness, tingling or burning in the face, neck and other areas, rapid, fluttering heartbeats (heart palpitations), chest pain, nausea, weakness. However, researchers have found no definitive evidence of a link between MSG and these symptoms. Researchers acknowledge, though, that a small percentage of people may have short-term reactions to MSG (Zeratsky, 2015). Other authors claim that the effects on the human body can be detrimental in large quantities (Baad-Hansen *et al.,* 2010; Olney, 1969).

The human desire for sweet products is innate. As previously stated, humans meet sweet taste already in breast milk. People naturally crave sweets and are searching for sweet foods since the beginnings or human history. Honey, for example, has been used since about 2000 BC. Over the past century, however, the most popular and most commonly used sweetener is sugar (sucrose). Commonly, it is believed that sugar is associated with many health complications and with lots of new diseases (mainly diabetes and obesity) (Kopelman, 2007). Therefore, during the recent decades, scientists have looked for its replacement. Sucrose, fructose, glucose-fructose syrups are not additives but natural ingredients and, therefore, have no E-number. Other sweeteners are produced synthetically. Already in 1878, saccharin was discovered, but began to be used only in the 1950s, mainly due to the historical and political situation. Substitute artificial sweeteners often cannot replace

Table 5.1. Common food colourings (http://understandingfoodadditives.org.uk/pages/Ch2p1-1.htm).

E Number	Name	Description
E100	Curcumin	Orange-yellow colour that is extracted from the roots of the turmeric plant.
E101	Riboflavin	Riboflavin is also known as vitamin B2. It can be obtained by fermenting yeast or synthesised artificially. In foods, it is used as an orange-yellow colour.
E102	Tartrazine	Yellow coloured synthetic azo dye. This colouring sparks controversy as some groups suggest it causes behavioural problems in children (see food issues).
E160a	β-carotene	Orange-yellow colour found in plants such as carrots, tomatoes and oranges.
E150a	Plain caramel	Dark brown to black colour. The most common colouring. 90% of all colouring used is caramel. Obtained by the heating of sugars.
E123	Amaranth	Dark purple coloured synthetic colour. Similar in colour to blackcurrants.

sugar and all its features. They are popular mainly due to their low energy level. In general, artificial sweeteners are divided into non-nutritive (high-intensity) and nutritive (zero-calorie) sweeteners. The most popular zero-calorie sweeteners are aspartame, acesulfame K, saccharin, and cyclamates, while the nutritive sweeteners are sorbitol, mannitol, and xylitol (Kozmonová, 2014). In addition to the artificial sweeteners, other sweet natural substitutes of sugar such as stevia, agave, maple syrup, etc., are also being used, and have caloric content.

Researchers from the Faculty of Biotechnology and Food Sciences (FBFS) of the Slovak University of Agriculture in Nitra (SUA) conducted research on this topic (Kozmonová, 2014); as an example, the authors compared the taste of various sweeteners used in green tea. Several types of sweeteners were used: sugar, honey, maple syrup, brown sugar, saccharin, cyclamate, aspartame, and stevia. The research showed that honey was the most delicious sweetener according to consumers, and it was assumed that honey was considered the healthiest alternative. Surprisingly, the stevia was found to be the least tasty sweetener; however, it is a healthy alternative to sugar. Stevia has a strong, but unpleasant taste which persisted for a long time. Besides, the author also concluded that natural sweeteners were preferred over artificial sweeteners.

A very similar conclusion has been reached by Rybanská *et al.* (2016) from the Faculty of Economics and Management (FEM) of Slovak University of Agriculture in Nitra. During a research conducted for a food company specialized in production of jams, new flavours were tested, according to company plans to introduce new products and tastes into the Slovak market. Instead of sugar, new jams contained natural fruit sugar (fructose) and had a greater proportion of fruit. Consumers were divided into two groups. One group tasted strawberry and blueberry jams, some sweetened with sugar and some with fructose, but they were not informed about that fact, they did not even have further information about jams. They identified as the tastiest samples, the ones sweetened with sugar. The second group tested the same jams, but they knew which jams were sweetened with fructose and which ones with sugar. They were also advised about healthy lifestyle and the benefits of natural sweeteners for human health. As a result, this group identified jams flavoured with fructose as tastier. Based on these results, it can be concluded that consumer preferences are strongly influenced by the information available to the consumers. In this case, a psychological effect has been aimed at protecting their own health and efforts to maintain a healthy lifestyle.

From a marketing point of view, taste research is getting not too much attention as compared to other senses. Of course, there are foods that everyone knows and most of the people like their taste. In particular, those are basic foods, such as bread, and butter. But because these foods are popular for most of the consumers and they like them and consider them absolutely necessary, their promotion is almost useless. Promotion is necessary for foods that are not common at the selling region. Nowadays, plenty of diverse food are easily available through the European market, mainly through supermarkets and hypermarkets. Until few years back people did not know them and thus did not crave to taste them. Those who did not travel might not even know that such products exist. For example, Slovak supermarkets nowadays offer food from all around the world. French sausages, Scandinavian meatballs, Turkish sweets, Greek cheese, Italian pasta, or South American specialties. For such products, it is essential to provide potential customers with some basic information about them to start knowing them and appreciating their quality. It is mainly curiosity what leads people to their first purchase. Many supermarkets use this curiosity to try new experiences and offer customers, for instance, thematic weeks: every week specialties from a different country are offered. Thus, with sufficient information, customers are willing to buy unusual products for the first time. But what to do when they do not like the taste the first time? How do you get them to repeated purchases of such products? It is a common practice that the sellers, operating in several countries, adjust what it is offered in their stores to the regional culture and preferences. Food products are selected to best match with the local customs and traditions. When the stores want to offer unusual products, for example within the thematic week, the selection consists of items that represent an interesting choice from the culture of the country of product origin, but are partially related to the products already available in the consumer country.

At this time, consumers are very interested in healthy lifestyle, health, beauty and harmony of body and soul. Thus, food products related to these facts are getting more and more popular in the market (especially organic foods). It is possible that they are not the most delicious, but are perceived as being beneficial for the health (often because of particularly good marketing or advertising campaigns), and therefore, they are widely sold and bought and are gradually becoming popular.

Tasting products directly in stores is becoming a popular tool for sales promotion, and it is also used to determine whether customers like the taste of products. In 1985, Johnson, Sommer and Martino conducted a research related to tasting food samples in 14 supermarkets (Johnson *et al.*, 1985), quietly watching customers who stopped to taste specific product samples and the authors found two main problems in the customers' behaviour. The first problem was that customers often used offered samples to fill their eating needs not to test whether they like the product and want to buy (some repeatedly returned or took more samples at one time). The second problem was the lack of hygiene because customers took the food with bare hands. Despite these shortcomings, product tasting can lead to more sales and it is relatively an inexpensive way of promoting sales. But it carries some risks too. If the customer finds out directly in the store that the offered product does not fit his/her preferences, he/she certainly would not buy it and will not recommend it and quickly forgets such product. Therefore, at present, besides the direct in-store tastings, adding small portions of the product to take away is also a common practice; in this way customer can taste the new product again when back at home.

Already in 1978, researchers (Steinberg and Yalch, 1978) examined purchasing behaviour of obese and non-obese customers. They recorded whether these customers were hungry or not and what happened when they taste a product in-store (namely pastries and donuts). With non-obese customers, the authors concluded that if they were hungry and tasted donuts in the store, samples were enough to alleviate their hunger and so they were willing to buy less as compared to non-obese customers who were hungry. With obese customers they found out that tasting the samples led to an increase in additional purchases and the level of hunger had minimal impact on purchasing behaviour. The authors believe that obese customers are accustomed to eat more, so a small sample did not satisfy their hunger, but highlighted characteristics of the food which ultimately lead to an increased shopping. Lindstrom (2011) did not distinguish between obese and non-obese customers, but reached similar conclusions. He found out that when the customers tried the product in store, it mostly filled them and were not willing to buy more. The author concluded that to increase the sales of a particular food product, it is ideal to combine this product with visual images. The most effective images were people eating, nicely arranged meals, dewy drinks, mouths biting sandwiches, cakes and other foods. If the customers do see such images, it brings out the feeling of hunger and they are willing to buy more. Lindstrom (2011) also conducted research in which people rated their satisfaction degree when looking at the pictures (not only the pictures of food). During the image viewing, various scents were injected into the room. If the smell corresponded with images (like a picture of a hamburger and a scent of fries), subjects rated more positively or better the picture. If the smell did not match the picture, then, the image was assessed more negatively. Because taste and smell are almost inseparable factors, it can be assumed that similar research with tastes would bring similar results; this is, that matching tastes with pictures will be evaluated more positively. Research at Department of Marketing and Trade of the FEM of SUA confirmed that the selected consumers evaluated more positively the taste of yogurt samples, when their packaging was considered more attractive.

Nowlis and Shiv (2005) examined the impact of disturbance on customers who were just in the process of tasting a product in the store. The authors found that distracting or amusing the customers during the tasting, increased sales of the tasted product. Participants tasted a food sample under high or low cognitive load, and subsequently evaluated the sampled item or chose between the item and an alternative one. Nowlis and Shiv (2005) explained this finding using a two-part model where the pleasure of tasting product is a function of the affective component. Affective component includes emotional responses and it is connected to a relatively automatic process. The information component is a more objective element of the product tasting experience, and it is associated with aspects such as the quality. The information component represents in greater part the controlled processes. Distracting the consumer affects his following selection by increasing the impact of affective component.

5.3.1 Is the combination of taste and smell a comprehensive sense?

> Taste is not just a matter of taste cells, because sensations that are evoked by the food play an important role in the smell. Our perception also affects the memory.

Experts are increasingly approaching the physiology of taste to the physiology of smell because the smell cannot be understood without the flavour. To bring this claim this test can be made: When you put strawberries in front of your nose, you feel that smells like strawberry, but until it is not chewed, you do not know how the taste will be. When the strawberry is chewed, you can find out that it has a strawberry flavour (tastes plus volatile compounds) that resembles the initial smell. However, if at that time you take a deep breath, then you do not feel the smell of strawberries anymore. Strawberry taste is described as sweet, slightly sour, with a crusty surface and soft inside (texture); later, other perceptions are drawn from the small grains of this fruit. All this information constitutes a very accurate picture of strawberries.

Smell is often featured as part of the taste without knowing why: the air that enters the mouth contains aromatic molecules of the strawberries, rising up into the nasal cavities, this is called 'retro-smell'. Other molecules stimulate the taste buds, so different tastes can be felt – this is the perception of the flavour, which is a combination of tastes and volatile molecules. But also the teeth are stimulated, together with the tongue, the gums and the jaw, supplying essential information for the global taste perception.

Annick Faurion of French National Centre for Scientific Research, Institut de Neurobiologie Alfred Fessard considers that this is a complex sense backed by sensations made possible by olfactory neurons. The key to decipher the taste is individual, as well as the smell and the taste cannot be summarized just to four or five basic categories.

The hypothesis that only four flavours exist is questioned by numerous scientific papers. Faurion based her criticism on a simple observation: if the same molecule was tasted by different people, it would be defined by some of them as sweet, while others would say it is salty or bitter (Faurion, 1980; Froloff *et al.*, 1996).

'In fact, sweet can be defined as the perception felt after eating sugar,' explains Faurion. The general term has been defined to talk about this feeling, but if it should be necessary to point out all the effects that sugar causes in the mouth, each would use a different word.

Unlike the smell, the taste is a very thorough sense, which is based on eight nerves and taste disorders are very rare. A frequent cause of this decline of this ability is the loss of a large number of teeth, smoking, certain medications and chemotherapy in the treatment of cancer (Pravda.sk, 2013).

5.4 Taste the success or does quality matter?

Taste is a sense that can work wonders, can attract, and win customers for life

In previous sections, authors have explained how the taste might affect consumer purchasing behaviour; it has been mentioned that the product does not have to be of the highest quality, even not to be expensive to be tasty and/or popular. It was also explained how additives and colours influence the consumers' taste, preference, and purchasing pattern. The taste, however, can also be affected by other factors. Therefore, the question is: how to achieve success on market?

As previously discussed (Rybanská *et al.*, 2016), it was found that if additional information is provided to consumers, they will evaluate differently the products and their taste perception and preference is different than if no information is provided and they only taste the products. From the following studies can be concluded that the taste of the product is greatly influenced by the product brand.

In 1964, Allison and Uhl conducted an experiment in which they asked consumers (who regularly drunk beer at least 3 times a week) to blind taste several types of beer. They found out that consumers were unable to distinguish their favourite brand. However, if the brands were identified, the taste of the consumer favourite beer brand was rated more positively. Similar results were found in the blank test of Pepsi Cola and Coca-Cola. In the blind taste tests, Pepsi Cola clearly prevailed, but if the consumers knew what they were drinking, they evaluated Coca-Cola better (Yglesias, 2013). Similar results were obtained by Bellizzi and Martin (1982), who found that the fact whether the product was manufactured by local or foreign company greatly affects the consumer preference of the products (domestic brands were rated more positively). Sprott and Shimp (2004) found that consumers evaluate more positive a known brand, sold nationwide, compared to brand names typical for a particular supermarket (store brands). The authors developed two theories to explain this experimental finding. If the customer wants to make a really good decision, it takes into account the external and internal characteristics of the product. If internal keys cannot be evaluated, then the consumer based its decision solely on the external keys. Therefore, if we provide customers the opportunity to taste the store brand product in the store, it will affect their decision. The second theory is called 'the congruity theory' (Mandler, 1982). According to this theory, a positive feeling to the brand is greater if a customer perceives only a slight mismatch between product categories. If there is a big difference between the products from the store brand and those of the famous brand, then, the feelings are less positive. Brands that are typical for particular supermarkets are not so trusted by customers as they are cheaper, however the quality might not be lower at all. Therefore, the supermarkets should allow sample tastings of their own products, because it could significantly increase their sales.

Studies dealing with blind taste tests and the relation between taste and brand also revealed that if the consumer does not know the brands, then it is willing to try a number of them, and most likely will choose the one with the highest quality. If the consumer knows a brand, it is willing to try less of the other brands and it will most likely choose the most famous brand, although its quality might not be the highest one.

McDaniel and Baker (1977) found that the package greatly affected the consumer preference of the product. They tested potato chips, first wrapped in a wax paper and, then, another sample in a 'new' polyvinyl packaging. In a blind test, consumers rated the consumer preference of potato chips as identical. However, if consumers were allowed to see the packaging, they favoured chips in polyvinyl package, although it was extremely hard to open. Lindstrom (2011) did similar research, where the packaging prominently impacted product sale. The subjects (women only) tested a low fat mayonnaise in two different packages. All women chose the mayonnaise in packaging that copied the feminine curves. No woman did choose the spherical container. Very similar results were achieved by Krishna and Morrin (2008), who came to the conclusion that the shape of the bottle of water affected its consumer preference.

All mentioned studies suggested that the product does not have to be the highest quality or most expensive to became the most popular one as there are plenty of factors that affect its perception, not only the taste but also consumer purchasing behaviour. A typical example of the popularity of low-quality meals is fast food. Who does not like fast food? Fast-food chains have usually very well developed marketing strategies and use the latest knowledge of marketing and largely sensory marketing. Their products appear more appealing mostly because of the combination of multiple sensory stimuli. The actual taste of food is intensified be the store scent and brightly coloured pictures showing nicely arranged dishes and happy people.

There are also foods that may not be the best or the tastiest, but are sold by well-known or even a luxury brands. Such dishes usually meet the highest quality specifications, but may not taste at all that good as related to their price. Finally, there are also very popular inexpensive and very tasty dishes that attract customers with their taste alone. A modest Chinese restaurant in Singapore serves the cheapest food in the world with the prestigious Michelin-star award. There are long lines waiting for traditional chicken with soy sauce, rice and noodles (Kovácsová, 2016). So, now you can get in Singapore food with Michelin-star for half the price of a Big Mac from the competition. This fact is appreciated in particular by the customers and this food is probably still the cheapest Michelin-starred food in the world.

Taste is a sense that can work wonders, can attract, and win customers for life. Sellers just need to learn to use it.

References

Allison, R.I. and Uhl, K.P., 1964. Influence of beer brand identification on taste perception. Journal of Marketing Research 1: 36-39.

Atkinson, R.L., Atkinson, R.C., Smith, E.E., Bem, D.J. and Nolen-Hoeksema, S., 2003. Psychologie. Portál, Prague, Czech Republic, 752 pp.

Baad-Hansen, L., Cairns, B., Ernberg, M. and Svennson, P., 2010. Effect of systemic monosodium glutamate (MSG) on headache and pericranial muscle sensitivity. Cephalalgia 30(1): 68-76.

Bellizzi, J.A. and Martin, W.S., 1982. The influence of national versus generic branding on taste perceptions. Journal of Business Research 10(3): 385-396.

Chandrashekar, J., Hoon, M.A., Ryba, J.P.N. and Zuker, Ch.S., 2006. The receptors and cells for mammalian taste. Nature 444: 288-294.

Collins, N., 2012. Babies could inherit sweet tooth in the womb. Available at: http://tinyurl.com/lgkdf8z.

Daly B.P., Daly, M.P., Minniti, N. and Daly, J.M., 2012. Sense of taste (Effect on behavior). In: Ramachandran, V.S. (ed.) Encyclopedia of human behaviour. Academic Press, San Diego, CA, USA, pp. 373-378.

Dunkel, A., Köster, J. and Hofmann, T., 2007. Molecular and sensory characterization of γ-glutamyl peptides as key contributors to the kokumi taste of edible beans. Journal of Agricultural and Food Chemistry 55: 6712-6719.

Faurion, A., Saito, S. and MacLeod, P., 1980. Sweet taste involves several distinct receptor mechanisms. Chemical Senses 5: 107-121.

Food additives: Colours, 2008. Available at: http://tinyurl.com/l6ny8yj.

Food additives: Flavourings, 2008. Available at: http://understandingfoodadditives.org.uk/pages/Ch2p3-1.htm.

Food additives: Sources of flavors, 2008. Available at: http://understandingfoodadditives.org.uk/pages/Ch2p3-3.htm.

Food additives: Why use additives? 2008. Available at: http://understandingfoodadditives.org.uk/pages/Ch2p0.htm.

Froloff, N., Faurion, A. and MacLeod, P., 1996. Multiple human taste receptor sites: a molecular modeling approach. Chemical Senses 21: 425-445.

Galindo, M.M., Voigt, N., Stein, J., Lengerich, J., Raguse, J.D., Hofmann, T., Meyerhof, W. and Behrens, M., 2011. G protein-coupled receptors in human fat taste perception. Chemical Senses 37(2): 123-139.

Horák, O., 2015. Phantom smell – when you perceive a flavor that does not exist in food. Available at: http://tinyurl.com/m3urqq9.

Hultén, B., 2011. Sensory marketing: the multi-sensory brand-experience concept. European Business Review 23(3): 256-273.

International Organization for Standardization, 2008. Terminology relating to the senses. Geneva, Switzerland. Available at: https://www.iso.org/obp/ui/#iso:std:iso:5492:ed-2:v1:en.

Jelen, H., 2011. Sensory and technological properties. CRC Press, Boca Raton, FL, USA, 504 pp.

Johnson, S.L., Sommer, R. and Martino, V., 1985. Consumer behavior at bulk food bins. Journal of Consumer Research 12(1): 114-117.

Kaneda, H., Maeshima, K., Goto, N., Kobayakawa, T., Ayabe-Kanamura, S. and Saito, S., 2000. Decline in taste and odor discrimination abilities with age, and relationship between gustation and olfaction. Chemical Senses 25: 331-337.

Kopelman, P., 2007. Health risks associated with overweight and obesity. Obesity Reviews 8(1): 13-17.

Kovácsová, L., 2016. Pouličný stánok dostal hviezdičku od Michelina, kura tam stojí dve eurá. Available at: http://tinyurl.com/nytmlrk.

Kozmonová, A., 2014. Analýza sladkej chuti prírodných a umelých sladidiel pomocou techniky merania intenzity v čase. Diplomová práca. SPU, Nitra, Slovak Republic, 61 pp.

Krishna, A. and Morrin, M., 2008. Does touch affect taste? The perceptual transfer of product container haptic cues. Journal of Consumer Research 34: 12.

Landis, B.N., Welge-Luessen, A., Brämerson, A., Bende, M., Mueller, C.A., Nordin, S. and Hummel, T., 2009. 'Taste Strips' – A rapid, lateralized, gustatory bedside identification test based on impregnated filter papers. Journal of Neurology 256: 242-248.

Laugerette, F., Gaillard, D., Passilly-Degrace, P., Niot, I. and Besnard, P., 2007. Do we taste fat? Biochemie 89: 265-269.

Lawless, H.T. and Heymann, H., 2010. Sensory evaluation of food. Principles of good practice. Springer, New York, NY, USA, pp. 57-77.

Lawrence, A., 1998. Understanding food additives. Chemical Industry Education Centre, Heslington, York, UK, 148 pp. Available at: http://tinyurl.com/n4ncamy.

Lindstrom, M., 2011. Brandwashed: tricks companies use to manipulate our minds and persuade us to buy. Crown Business, New York, NY, USA, 304 pp.

Mandler, G., 1982. The structure of value: accounting for taste. In: Clark, M.S. and Fiske S.T. (eds.) Affect and cognition: the 17th annual symposium. Erlbaum, Hillsdale, NJ, USA, pp. 3-36.

McDaniel, C. and Baker, R.C., 1977. Convenience food packaging and the perception of product quality. Journal of Marketing 41(4): 57.

Methevn, L., Allen, V.J., Withers, C.A. and Gosney, M.A., 2012. Ageing and taste. Nutrition Society 71: 556-565.

Mirmiran, P., Fazeli, M.R., Asghari, G., Shafiee, A. and Azizi, F., 2010. Effect of pomegranate seed oil on hyperlipidaemic subjects: a double-blind placebo-controlled clinical trial. British Journal of Nutrition 104(3): 402-406.

Mojet, J., Heidema, J. and Christ-Hazelhof, E., 2003. Taste perception with age: generic or specific losses in supra-threshold intensities of five taste qualities? Chemical Senses 28(5): 397-413.

Ninomiya, K., 1998. Natural occurrence. Food Reviews International 14(2-3): 177-211.

Nowlis, S.M. and Shiv, B., 2005. The influence of consumer distractions on the effectiveness of food-sampling programs. Journal of Marketing Research 42(2): 157.

Olney, J.W., 1969. Brain lesions, obesity, and other disturbances in mice treated with monosodium glutamate. Available at: https://www.ncbi.nlm.nih.gov/pubmed/5778021.

Pravda.sk., 2013. Is taste and smell a comprehensive sense? Available at: http://tinyurl.com/l4arqcb.

Seo, H.S. and Hummel, T., 2011. Auditory-olfactory integration: congruent or pleasant sounds amplify odor pleasantness. Chemical Senses 36: 301-309.

Smith, D.V. and Margolskee, R.F., 2001. Making sense of taste. Scientific American 284: 32-39.

Sprott, D.E. and Shimp, T.A., 2004. Using product sampling to augment the perceived quality of store brands. Journal of Retailing 80: 305-315.

Steinberg, S.A. and Yalch, R.F., 1978. When eating begets buying: the effects of food samples on obese and nonobese shoppers. Journal of Consumer Research 4(4): 243-246.

Rybanská, J., Nagyová, Ľ. and Kubeláková, A., 2016. Sensory marketing strategy: use of the sense of taste on the global market of food. Globalization and its socio-economic consequences. Žilinská Univerzita, Žilina, Slovak Republic, pp. 1912-1918.

The Food Additives and Ingredients Association and The Chemical Industry Education Centre. 2005. Food additives: Colours. Available at: http://understandingfoodadditives.org.uk/pages/Ch2p1-1.htm.

The Food Additives and Ingredients Association and The Chemical Industry Education Centre. 2005. Food additives: Flavourings. Available at: http://understandingfoodadditives.org.uk/pages/Ch2p3-1.htm.

The Food Additives and Ingredients Association and The Chemical Industry Education Centre. 2005. Food additives: Sources of flavors. Available at: http://understandingfoodadditives.org.uk/pages/Ch2p3-3.htm.

The Food Additives and Ingredients Association and The Chemical Industry Education Centre. 2005. Food additives: Why use additives? Available at: http://understandingfoodadditives.org.uk/pages/Ch2p0.htm.

Topky.sk. 2012. Mother´s food choices *during pregnancy* influence what *child* likes to *eat* after birth, 2012. Available at: http://www.topky.sk/cl/13/1300745/Vyskum--Detom-chuti-to--co-ich-matky-jedli-v-tehotenstve-.

Tordoff, M.G. and Sandell, M.A., 2009. Vegetable bitterness is related to calcium content. Appetite 52: 498-504.

Velasco, C., Woods, A.T., Petit, O., Cheok, A.D. and Spence, C., 2016. Crossmodal correspondences between taste and shape, and their implications for product packaging: a review. Food Quality and Preference 52: 17-26.

Yamamoto, K. and Ishimaru, Y., 2012. Oral and extra-oral taste perception. Seminars in Cell and Developmental Biology 24: 240-246.

Yglesias, M., 2013. Sweet sorrow. Coke won the cola wars because great taste takes more than a single sip. Available at: http://tinyurl.com/klpv48r.

Zeratsky, K., 2015. What is MSG? Is it bad for you? Available at: http://tinyurl.com/nsl6wp7.

6. The sense of touch

D.B. López Lluch[1]* and L. Noguera Artiaga[2]

[1]Universidad Miguel Hernández de Elche, Escuela Politécnica Superior de Orihuela, Department of Agri-Environmental Economics, Sociology and Agricultural Policy, Ctra. Beniel, km 3.2, 03312 Orihuela, Alicante, Spain; [2]Universidad Miguel Hernández de Elche, Escuela Politécnica Superior de Orihuela, Department of Agro-Food Technology, Ctra. Beniel, km 3.2, 04 Orihuela, Alicante, Spain; david.lopez@umh.es

Abstract

In this chapter, we will try to understand what touch is, which implications it can have in sensory marketing, and how it can affect product and business definitions. The sense of touch is one of the central forms of perceptual experience. Positive touch from others is necessary for an individual's healthy development. Often ignored when we talk about our fundamental senses, the sensation of touch is a fundamental part of our daily experience, influencing what we buy, who we love and even how we heal. We use this sense to gather information about our surroundings and as a means of establishing trust and social bonds with other people. Vision and smell alone are not always enough for consumers to evaluate products or to make purchase decisions, and including other important information, such as on the form, robustness, texture or weight of a product perceived by the sense of touch (or tactile sense) for sure will help. Visual and tactile senses can be identified as the most active of our five senses. In retail management practice, it is obvious that the tactile sense, as a sensory channel, is significant in purchase and consumption processes for goods such as cars, computers, clothing, home equipment, mobile phones, shoes or for restaurant services. The question of whether merely touching an object influences a consumer's perception of ownership and the amount they are willing to pay for an object has not been investigated in depth. In this chapter, we will look into these points: (1) how does touch affect retail and selling; (2) how could touch affect the value of products; and (3) touch opportunities for branding.

Keywords: tactile sense, ownership, retail, selling, value, branding

Esther Sendra and Ángel A. Carbonell-Barrachina (eds.) **Sensory and aroma marketing**
DOI 10.3920/978-90-8686-841-4_6, © Wageningen Academic Publishers 2017

6.1 Introduction

Without touch, it would be difficult to be alive in our world

Touch is a perception resulting from activation of neural receptors, generally in the skin including hair follicles, but also in the tongue, throat, and mucosa. A variety of pressure receptors respond to variations in pressure (firm, brushing, sustained, etc.).

Touch is also the first sense to develop in the womb and the last sense one loses with age. Even before we are born, we start responding to touch and also start touching ourselves.

During pregnancy, the senses develop in the following order; touch, smell, taste, audition, and then vision. Touch lets the human embryo learn its place in the womb and find itself. The touch sensation first develops around the mouth area and then proceeds downwards from head to toe. Mark Lythgoe, a neuroscientist at the Institute of Child Health has used Magnetic Resonance Imaging to show that at 8 weeks of gestation, a human embryo can respond to being touched on the cheek; at 12 weeks, it can begin to suck its thumb and lick; and, at 32 weeks of gestation, it can feel and comprehend temperature, pressure, and pain. Other research shows that receptor cells on the skin develop at 20 weeks, and that at 24 weeks the embryo has a weak grasp which turns into a firm grasp at 26 weeks, so that it will hold anything placed in its palm including the umbilical cord. The reversal, loss of sensory acuity, seems to be faster and earlier for vision, audition, smell, and taste as compared to touch (Krishna, 2012).

Touch is a fundamental form of non-visual perception, one that plays a crucial role in nearly all of our sensory experiences. It is, unlike many of the other senses, more plausibly taken to be inherently multisensory, given the diversity of its constituent systems and forms of experience (Fulkerson, 2011).

Without touch, it would be difficult to be alive in our world. Many of our feelings would not exist: feet hitting the floor when walking, no sensation when something sharp cut us, etc. Furthermore, any movement requires a fine awareness of our body. This is possible through proprioception, an internal form of tactile sense (Fulkerson, 2011).

There is a huge amount of information received about the world through the sense of touch. However, most of the key processes about how the skin perceives touch are still unknown.

The skin is the barrier between our internal body systems and the outside world. Its ability to perceive touch sensations gives our brains a wealth of information about the environment around us, such as temperature, pain, and pressure. The somatic sensory system is responsible for the sense of touch. This system has nerve receptors that help to feel when something comes into contact with our skin (Figure 6.1). These sensory receptors are generally known as touch receptors or pressure receptors. We also have nerve receptors that feel pain and temperature changes, such as hot and cold (Fulkerson, 2012).

The loss or impairment of the ability to feel anything touched is called tactile anesthesia. Paresthesia is a sensation of tingling, pricking, or numbness of the skin that may result from nerve damage and may be permanent or temporary (Fulkerson, 2012).

There are several basic kinds of touch that we may experience (Cicero, 2009):

▸ Intimate, our pressure receptors respond to a handshake, hug or kiss. If the person giving the touch is someone we care about, we will probably feel warm and comforted. Our pressure sensors send the feeling of how hard the embrace is, and our brain interprets the nature of the touch as soothing.

▸ Healing or therapeutic, this type of touch is often associated with massage or acupuncture. Sometimes, the pressure is gentle and meant to soothe sore muscles. Other times, the pressure is deep to work out knots. Despite differences in severity of pressure, we are likely to be aware that the outcome is healing, so our body allows us to relax.

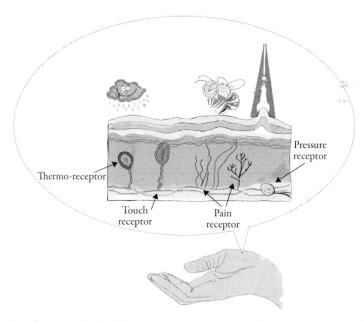

Figure 6.1. Our skin is packed with many sense receptors. Each type responds to different sensations (image: José Antonio Granero Vicente).

- ► Exploratory or inquisitive, we all learn about the world through our sense of touch. Many people test out foods, fabrics or other objects by feeling different textures. Sometimes it is possible to rely solely on the sense of touch. This is why it is easy for us to reach into our bag and find a pair of keys without looking. We know the cold feeling of the metal key and hard smooth feel of our plastic key chain.
- ► Aggressive or painful, we all know that touch can also equate to pain if the pressure is too much and the intent is wrong. A handshake that is too firm can be uncomfortable instead of reassuring.

As early as the 4th century BC, Aristotle proposed his theory of *aisthesis* or sensation which suggests that our five senses are ordered hierarchically, with 'touch' on top, and the other senses increasing the acuity of the touch sensation. For Aristotle, touch provided a true picture of the intrinsic nature of the object, so that the soft coat of a kitten would be indicative of its innate softness of character. Also, touch and the cosmos were connected because sexual stimulation worked through the sense of touch allowing the human race to continue (Krishna, 2012).

Aristotle noted that touch, unlike the other dominant modalities, seemingly lacked a single 'proper sensible'. On this account, a proper sensible is a sensory feature only available in a single modality, one that was constitutive of that modality. For vision, colour is the proper sensible. Any experience of colour is visual, because no other modality provides awareness of that feature. The proper sensibles were contrasted with the common sensibles found in more than one modality. Touch does not have a single plausible proper sensible. Instead it has multiple potential proper sensibles, including pressure and temperature; this too might be a strong reason for treating touch as a collection of distinct senses rather than a single modality (Fulkerson, 2016).

In this chapter, we will try to understand what touch is, which implications it can have in sensory marketing, and how it can affect to product and business definition.

6.2 Does touch matter?

Desire for touch is stronger than any other desire

The sense of touch is one of the central forms of perceptual experience. A hug from a loved one can lower our blood pressure and make us feel valued and important. A firm handshake with a friend can create a connection. How we perceive the hug or handshake, along with how our touch receptors receive the pressure, is rooted in our brain (Gallace and Spence, 2010).

Positive touch from others is necessary for an individual's healthy development. Often ignored when we talk about our fundamental senses, the sensation of touch is a fundamental part of our daily experience, influencing what we buy, who we love and even how we heal. We use this sense to gather information about our surroundings and as a means of establishing trust and social bonds with other people (Fulkerson, 2014b).

The organization of the body's touch circuits powerfully influences our lives, affecting everything from consumer choice to sexual intercourse, from tool use to the origins of language, and from chronic pain to healing. Interpersonal touch is crucial to social bonding and individual development. Sensory and emotional context work together to distinguish between perceptions of what feels good and what feels bad (Linden, 2016).

Touch is, in several ways, seemingly different from the other senses. For one thing, touch does not seem to have a single sense organ. The skin, of course, is the most plausible candidate sensory organ, but the skin itself is not sensory. Instead, the skin contains many different sensory systems. Many of them, like those that code for pain and itch, do not seem to be tied directly to the sense of touch. For instance, we do not, at least in most contexts, seem to treat cutaneous pains as part of the touch sense. The same seems true for itch, tingles, and twinges, though perhaps these seem closely tied with touch. At any rate, they are not paradigm instances of tactual perception, and if they seem more closely tied to touch, then, this is something in need of explanation (Fulkerson, 2016).

Touch seems to have both passive and active nature. In its more passive forms, touch involves cutaneous activations across the surface of the body. These include bodily sensations of hot and cold, pressure, and vibration. In addition, these activations have a limited, entirely bodily spatial character. On the other hand, we use every part of our bodies to actively explore the environment. We use our hands, arms and fingers, we move our trunks and legs, and we actively feel with nearly every surface of our body. Touch in ordinary use involves specialized movements and grips. Haptic touch involves feedback from our movements, along with information from our motor activities (both in motor planning and efference copies) (Fulkerson, 2016).

Perhaps most importantly, it also includes information from receptors in our muscles and joints. All of these elements interact and play a critical role in forming and developing our sense of touch. For this reason, touch, especially of the active, haptic variety, seems like an ideal model for views of perception according to which perception is essentially a form of action, or at least a form of experience that involves action in a unique manner (Fulkerson, 2016).

Even if we focus only on those systems usually associated with touch, we find a number of distinct sensory channels. Some of these have proven incredibly difficult to isolate and study. Indeed, we are just now starting to understand the role and function of the most basic receptor types involved in touch. Another methodological challenge concerns the deep connection between touch and exploratory activities. For touch, many of the historically important empirical investigations have focused on cutaneous touch, especially on mapping the two-point threshold over the extent of the body. This threshold is the minimal distance at which a subject can discriminate two distinct stimuli (Figure 6.2). Its study requires subjects to remain completely still, while very small probes (like horse hair) are used to generate stimuli. It is much more difficult to measure touch in ecologically salient contexts where there are unconstrained movements using the whole body (Fulkerson, 2016).

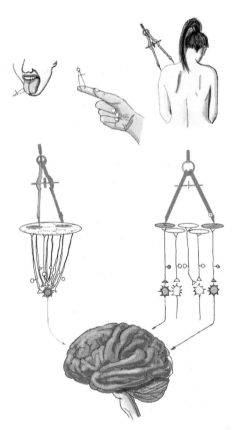

Figure 6.2. Two-point discrimination test: many primary sensory neurons converging onto a single secondary neuron creates a very large receptive field. When fewer neurons converge, secondary receptive field are much smaller and the stimuli are perceived as distinct stimuli (image: José Antonio Granero Vicente).

The importance of touch for humans has been demonstrated in many studies. Drastic examples of young children who have been deprived of touch and have suffered as a result the devastating consequences of touch deprivation. However, there is still not much research on the consequences of touch deprivation in later childhood and adulthood. 'If you do not get touch right after you are born, all kinds of terrible things happen, and not just cognitive and emotional, your immune system does not develop properly, your digestive system tends to have problems; there is a whole rack of health problems that can develop if you do not receive touch in early life' (Linden, 2016).

In the 1950s, parenting manuals advised parents not to touch their children too much, recommending, instead of hugs and kisses, giving kids a 'pat on the head'. However, Linden (2016) warns that touch deprivation denies children a chance to become socially integrated with the people around them. 'A parent's touch is very crucial for a child's development,' 'it is not optional'.

For instance, research has looked at what an infant desires more a mother's touch or basic nutrition? During the 1950s, the psychologist Harry Harlow conducted studies of the effects of isolation on infant monkeys. He separated monkeys at birth from their parents and siblings, keeping them in clean cages with adequate food. He, then, put two 'surrogate' mothers in the cages. One was a wire mother with a milk bottle and one was a wooden mother covered in terrycloth without a milk bottle. The comforting surrogate cloth mother and the nurturing surrogate wire mothers were created by placing a 100 W light bulb behind the cloth mother and attaching a bottle with milk to the wire mother. The cloth mom provided comfort through contact, and the monkeys chose her over the nutrition mom. The infant monkeys clung desperately onto the terrycloth mothers for hours, ignoring the desire for food in exchange for the softness of the terry cloth (Hatfield, 1994). This demonstrates that the desire for touch is stronger than any other desire, and implies that mother-infant bonding is more dependent on affectionate touch than on the fact that the mother provides food to the infant.

The touch deprived monkeys, in Harlow's studies, experienced stereotypic abnormalities in their development and behaviour. These monkeys engaged in self-clasping and rocking behaviours and were disinterested in their environment. They avoided socializing with other monkeys, were timid, and disliked being touched. When they did interact with other monkeys they were very aggressive. They had difficulty finding sexual partners, often were unable to mate properly, and abused their mates and offspring (Hatfield, 1994).

In the years since Harlow's studies of monkeys, other researchers have conducted further studies on the effect of touch deprivation on development. The current consensus is that adequate affectionate touch is necessary for an individual's proper development (Leonard, 2009).

Monkeys preferred to stay close to a surrogate cloth mother than a wire mother where the cloth mother provides warmth and the wire mother provides nutrition. Similar comfort through physical contact has been shown in human infants, where holding, caressing, cradling, or massaging the baby, that is, touching the baby, has been shown to enhance parent-infant attachment and also enhance the baby's emotional and physiological health (Montagu, 1971).

But, does everyone have the same need for contact or touch? When it comes to social situations, the primary purpose of touch is to forge trust and cooperation. Friendly touch communicates to someone.

Research has found that players on sports teams that have lots of celebratory touch tend to perform better, while studies have also shown that in a romantic relationship, touch (both sexual and non-sexual) is enormously important. Touch is the glue that makes social bonds (Linden, 2016).

So what is happening in the brain and body when we experience a warm touch of a loved one? The touch stimulates C-fibres [a type of nerve fibre which Linden (2016) refers to as 'caress sensors'] that convey information to the brain about interpersonal touch, specifically, the light caress. These fibres send signals to the posterior insula (a brain area involved in perception and motor control), which produces a soft, pleasant sensation (Fulkerson, 2014c).

A final area of increasing philosophical investigation concerns the role of pleasure and pain in perception, something typically referred to as 'affect'. The question is central to our full understanding of the richness and complexity of perceptual experience. While perception is often assumed to be entirely receptive and descriptive, it is just as often evaluative and motivational. When we smell something awful or see something graphic, we have intense reactions to these experiences, and are directly motivated to act in various ways. These forms of affective perceptual experience seemingly bridge the gap between experience, emotion, and evaluative judgment. For these reason, there are many importantly different accounts available for explaining the nature of these experiences (Fulkerson, 2016).

Touch again is an excellent source for such investigation. Our tactual experiences often seem to have a felt pleasant or unpleasant character. This is not simply an associated but distinct state of pleasure or pain that accompanies the perceptual experience, but part of the perceptual experience itself. Paradigm examples include the pleasure derived from delicious food or the awfulness of certain bad smells.

Researchers have discovered a specialized class of afferent nerve channels that seem to be responsible for the experience of pleasantness (Löken *et al.*, 2009; McGlone *et al.*, 2012).

These channels, called CT-afferents, are maximally responsive to slow, regular activations such as those generated by a feather pulled gently across the arm. These channels seem pleasant versions of the famous C-fibres implicated in pain experiences. While the discovery of these afferents has been an exciting development in our understanding of affective perceptual experience, they also raise many questions. How can a receptor 'code for pleasantness'? Are there other similar receptors for pleasant touch in glabrous skin (the smooth, hairless skin of the lips and palms where they are no CT-afferents)? What do these receptors mean for our understanding of pleasure and pain and affective experience more generally? And returning to where we started, we can seriously wonder whether and to what extent the CT system seems to be a part of touch. The CT system seems, unlike that for cutaneous pain, to be a genuine component of the touch system; on the other hand, the CT system also does not appear to have any direct discriminative function. CT interactions reveal much about the complex ways in which emotions and motivation can come to be closely connected to perceptual experience (Fulkerson, 2014a).

They can also be seen as a bridge to a better understanding of affiliative touch, the close form of caring touch that forms an essential element of social bonding and human development, especially of the immune system (Field, 2003).

Peck and Childers (2003) have identified individual differences in an individual's motivation or preference to touch. The 'Need for Touch' (NFT) is conceptually defined as a preference for the extraction and utilization of information obtained through the touch or the haptic system. This need to examine products haptically is driven by two different motivations associated with either 'consumer problem solvers' or consumers seeking 'fun, fantasy, arousal, sensory stimulation, and enjoyment.' In the utilitarian view, consumers are concerned with purchasing products in an efficient and timely manner to achieve their goals with a minimum of irritation. The NFT scale is conceptualized as a multidimensional construct with two underlying factors: (1) an instrumental factor; and (2) an autotelic factor.

6.3 Reach out and touch the business

Touching an object results in an increase in perceived ownership of that object

According to Hultén (2012), the sense of sight is considered the most important sensory channel for perceiving a commercial environment, and research confirms the impact of visual cues on consumer behaviour in terms of consumption, purchase quantity or sale. The sense of smell is another important sensory channel, and a number of studies (Hultén, 2012) have shown that olfactory cues have a significant impact on consumer behaviour in retail settings. However, vision and smell alone are not always enough for consumers to evaluate products or to make purchase decisions, and omit other important information, such as on the form, robustness, texture or weight of a product, that the sense of touch (or tactile sense) might communicate. Visual and tactile senses can be identified as the most active of our five senses. In retail management practice, it is obvious that the tactile sense, as a sensory channel, is significant in purchase and consumption processes for goods such as cars, computers, clothing, home equipment, mobile phones, shoes or for restaurant services.

There are significant differences between shoppers' touching behaviour in a manipulated point-of-purchase compared to a conventional one. These findings show that visual and olfactory sensory cues have a positive impact on shoppers' touching behaviour, purchase intentions and total sale. Sensory cues exert a positive impact on consumers' desire to touch. Sensory cues frame consumers' affective responses and decision making through involving the sense of touch (Hultén, 2012).

Merely touching an object results in an increase in perceived ownership of that object. For non-owners, or buyers, perceived ownership can be increased with either mere touch or with imagery encouraging to touch. The perceived ownership can also be increased through touch for legal owners, or sellers of an object. Valuation of an object is jointly influenced by both the perceived ownership and by the valence of the touch experience (Peck and Shu, 2009).

If a product category varies in a diagnostic way on one or more of its attributes, consumers will be more motivated to touch the product prior to purchase to check specific attribute information. Furthermore, examining specific instrumental product information through touch and finding the experience of touching a pleasantly valenced object can influence persuasion, even if the touch element provides no information regarding the product (Peck and Wiggins, 2006).

Research has established that consumers like to evaluate products and gather information about them through touch (McCabe and Nowlis, 2003). It has also been suggested that it should be advantageous for retailers to let consumers touch and interact with products in retail settings (Grohmann *et al.*, 2007). Studies have also shown that consumers prefer store environments that allow them to inspect products physically (Krishna and Morrin, 2008) and to pick up, touch, and choose among products that are displayed (McCabe and Nowlis, 2003).

However, the question of whether merely touching an object influences a consumer's perception of ownership and the amount they are willing to pay for an object has not been investigated in depth.

Let's have a look, in the following sections, into two questions, and an opportunity:
▸   How does touch affect retail and selling?
▸   How could touch affect the value of products? and
▸   Touch opportunities for branding.

6.3.1 Touch and retailing

In retailing, store atmospherics emphasise the sensory qualities of a service scape, often designed and formulated to attract customer interest and response, as well as to generate a positive retail experience in a B2C (business to consumer) or B2B (business to business) context (Noad and Rogers, 2008). As with sensory stimuli, displays, colours, employees, lighting, music, or scents, atmospheric cues are intended to create positive emotions and increase sales through appealing human senses (Soars, 2009).

Moreover, atmospheric cues are significant for a hedonic retail experience in terms of attractive stimuli and facilitating stimuli (Ballantine *et al.*, 2010). The term 'atmospherics' is a way of describing a commercial environment and its physical factors, distinguishing among the aural, olfactory, tactile, and visual dimensions of a store. In the definition of an atmosphere, the human senses play a major role, and the store atmosphere is described in sensory terms. In this regard, sight, sound, scent, and touch are the major sensory channels. A general assumption from research is that ambient stimuli with background elements should appeal to the five human senses (sight, sound, smell, touch, and taste), thus being appealing to and attracting customers. Various studies have also demonstrated the impact of retail atmospherics on consumer behaviour (Hultén, 2012).

Ever since the 1950s, research has focused on the 'personalities' associated with the physical attributes of retail outlets through the concept of retail atmospherics. Previous research has shown that five major elements of retail atmospherics, namely: (1) exterior; (2) interior; (3) layout; (4) point of purchase; and (5) human variables, lay the ground for consumer interactions, experiences and the store image of retail settings. It has also been suggested that retail atmospherics may influence consumers' current store behaviour, as well as their future store behaviour (Hultén, 2012).

Previous research in marketing has examined product category differences and found that some product categories encourage touch more than others. In this sense, Grohmann *et al.* (2007) found that retailers can benefit from allowing customers to touch their products. They found that tactile input influences product evaluations and that the need for touch impacted product evaluations, when tactile input was available in single, but not multiple, product evaluations. In four experiments, Grohmann *et al.* (2007), effects of tactile input were observed for product categories wherein tactile input was diagnostic, and depended on product quality. While this effect was moderated by individual differences in need for touch when there was no opportunity for multiple product comparisons, there was no support for a mediating role of affect. According to this, retailers are advised to allow consumers to touch products in retail environments, because such a strategy results in more favourable consumer responses. In addition to the increased likelihood of choice of tactilely diagnostic products in physical retail environments, and increased consumer confidence in evaluations input, evaluations are positively affected, particularly if product quality levels are high although retailers may be inclined to prevent consumers from touching high quality merchandise in particular (e.g. due to concerns regarding theft or damage of merchandise or increased costs of keeping touchable items in good condition). In the case of foods, avoiding food safety concerns may be a good reason to discourage touch.

McCabe and Nowlis (2003) found that many consumers purchase products in stores, where they can physically examine and touch the items. In addition, consumers shop for products online or through direct mail, where they cannot physically examine and touch the merchandise. Building on an analysis of perceptual mechanisms involved in the sense of touch, they saw that products with primarily material properties, such as clothing or carpeting, are more likely to be preferred in shopping environments that allow physical inspection than in those environments that do not. There is no difference in preference across the two environments for products with primarily geometric properties, such as packaged goods, for which vision is highly diagnostic. Furthermore, when the touch properties of a material product are verbally described, this reduces the difference in preference between the two environments.

Peck and Childers (2003) found that haptic information, or information attained through touch by the hands, is important for the evaluation of products that vary in terms of material properties related to texture, hardness, temperature, and weight (Figure 6.3). The authors develop and propose a conceptual framework to illustrate that salience of haptic information differs significantly across products, consumers, and situations. The authors use two experiments to assess how these factors interact to impair or enhance the acquisition and use of haptic information. Barriers to touch, such as a retail display case, can inhibit the use of haptic information and consequently decrease confidence in product evaluations and increase the frustration level of consumers, who are more motivated to touch products. In addition, written descriptions and visual depictions of products can partially enhance acquisition of certain types of touch information.

The sense of touch excels at obtaining texture, hardness, temperature, and weight information (Klatzky and Lederman, 1992, 1993). According to Spence *et al.* (2014), in-store temperature has prompted relatively little research. In one study, though, researchers measured the temperature in a cross-section of Manhattan stores (e.g. Bergdorf, Macy's, Temperatures varied as a function of the price of the merchandise: the higher the price point, the colder the air conditioning in the store. This might be a sensible strategy given recent research showing that colder ambient temperatures tend to lead to more emotional decision making and greater preference for hedonic options while warmer stores lead to more cognitive decision making and greater preference for utilitarian options. Moreover, this research finds that customers use these models of decision making to achieve an optimal temperature, or what we might think of as an optimal level of thermal stimulation.

Figure 6.3. Consumer choosing vegetables in a local market based her choice on tactile sensations.

Touching products has been shown to exert a positive impact on shopper attitudes and behaviour, as well as on purchase intentions (Citrin *et al.*, 2003; Peck and Wiggins, 2006), and it is associated with effective product placement in stores. Moreover, research has demonstrated that for some people, the effects of touch are stronger than for others (Peck and Childers, 2003).

It is also evident that positive affective responses impact on attitudes and behaviour. By using touch, a positive affective response might result in more positive attitudes toward a product (Peck and Wiggins, 2006). In this regard, touch means acquiring knowledge about the product and its characteristics, such as form, hardness, texture or weight. They also point out that touch has potentially significant implications for store atmospherics, in the form of in-store and point-of-purchase displays. Researchers claim that displays should encourage touch and result in an interaction with products that customers would otherwise have ignored. This could increase impulse and unplanned purchases (Hultén, 2012).

6.3.2 Increase in the value of products by touching

Research on retailing reveals a paucity of knowledge on how visual and olfactory sensory cues impact on consumer touch behaviour. Touch behaviour has been overlooked in research, despite the fact that consumers use this sense to obtain information about products and become frustrated if they are unable to touch them (Citrin *et al.*, 2003; Peck and Childers, 2003). Moreover, research has shown that touch has a positive impact on consumer attitudes, behaviour and purchase intentions (Peck and Wiggins, 2006). However, the knowledge of its role in consumer decision making remains limited (Peck and Childers, 2003); thus, there is a real need to investigate touch behaviour in greater depth.

Haptic information has been demonstrated to impact persuasion in several ways. The ability to touch a product has been shown to increase positive attitudes and purchase intentions toward products that possess instrumental touch attributes such as the material properties of texture and softness (Grohmann *et al.*, 2007; Peck and Childers, 2003).

The need for haptic information in product evaluation has been linked to the placement of products in stores and to the failure of certain products to be successfully sold online. A taxonomy of touch in consumer behaviour delineates two forms of touch that consumers engage in: (1) instrumental touch, which is related to the use of touch to ascertain specific haptic attributes when a purchase goal is salient; and (2) hedonic touch, in which the goal of the shopper is to enjoy the sensory experience, often without a product purchase goal (Peck and Johnson, 2011).

Twenty-five years of research have shown that consumers' valuation of an object increases once they have taken ownership of it; a finding commonly known as the endowment effect. The effect has been replicated in a variety of settings and with a variety of objects, including lottery tickets, mugs, pens, and chocolate bars. One feature of nearly all endowment effect experiments is that the buyers (non-owners) and sellers (owners) have the opportunity to physically hold the object being traded. In the endowment literature, no previous work has directly considered whether the actual object touch, inherent in these studies, influences the perception of ownership and the valuation of the object (Shu and Peck, 2011).

Touch does affect perceived ownership, and the object valuation literature, by introducing new measures that operate as mediators. While ownership is considered to be critical to the endowment effect, it has generally been manipulated in prior endowment studies through legal ownership with sellers, who own the object, and buyers, who do not (Peck and Shu, 2009).

6.3.3 Touch opportunities for branding

Fiorini (2015) in her thesis 'autotelic vs instrumental need for touch: empirical evidence from a field study' made a deep study about tactile marketing.

Touch is likely to offer numerous opportunities for innovative branding and marketing in the years to come. Some companies are even going further and considering the practicalities associated with trademarking the signature feel of their brands to help distinguish them from the competition at a more emotional and/or affective level (Lindstrom, 2005).

Most firms tried to create an identity image around a product in terms of tactile marketing. Companies are trying to give their product and packages a surface feel that is multisensory congruent with the overall brand image (Gallace and Spence, 2011). For example, a few years ago, the manufacturers of 'Velvet' toilet tissue packaged their product in a protective plastic wrapping that had been specially treated to give it something of the feel of real velvet; thus, ensuring that the tactile feel of the product packaging was semantically congruent with the overall brand (Gallace and Spence, 2011).

The touch experience is of a lot of importance in purchasing and consuming services. This fact is often recognized; for example, through the soft chairs for comfort at a travel company and through the hard chairs and tables at a fast food restaurant.

Also, the hardness of the floor has been shown to be determinant on product valuation and retail brand perception (Möller and Herm, 2013). Customer experiences play an important role in retail brand management. This research investigated how bodily experiences in retail environments influence customers' perceptions of retail brand personalities. Based on research on human personality perception, they proposed that bodily experiences transfer metaphoric meaning to customers' brand perceptions. In a field experiment and a lab experiment they manipulated participants' bodily experiences (feeling of hardness and temperature) and consistently found a metaphor-specific transfer of experiences to retail brand personality perceptions (on the dimensions 'ruggedness' and 'warmth'). Another study revealed the mechanism behind the effect and demonstrates concept activation elicited by bodily experiences in customers' minds. The results replicated the previous findings that bodily experiences transfer in a metaphoric way to perceptions of retail brand personalities. Participants in the warmer environment perceived retail brands to be warmer than participants in the cooler room. The findings of this research have both theoretical implications for retail branding and practical implications for retailing management.

Companies need to consider how does the consumer's touch feel their product and brand and the subsequent emotions evoked. Clear objectives to cognitive contents must be established to communicate them via the sense of touch. Once the message to be communicated by touch has been defined, the challenge becomes in choosing those tactile sensations that are best suited to delivering that concept of the product (Gallace and Spence, 2014).

Brands can be classified through tactile sense expressions, such as material and surface in product and service landscapes, and also through temperature and weight. For example, heavy objects are often associated with high quality; other important sense expressions are form and stability. Lindstrom (2005) discussed the Coca Cola's use of the nostalgic glass bottle to reinforce its brand image and suggested that the main point behind this selection was the tactile sensation (consumers feel comfortable with the form and stability of the bottle in their hand, and associate this comfort with the brand).

The importance of the tactile aspects of packaging design comes from the effect of the reintroduction of the traditional Coke bottle: reports in the consumer target market suggested that sales increased by 12%, attributable in part to the reintroduction of Coke's signature contour bottle (Gallace and Spence, 2011).

However, it has been argued that is the 'sight' of the shaped bottle to be determinant in purchase, rather than the feel of its distinctive shape. This is reiterated by the presence of the image of the bottle on cans and advertising. Also, Spence and Gallace (2011) concluded that most experiments found that in situations of intersensory conflict, the vision dominates over touch, when evaluating the shape of an object. However, this is complemented through the people's need to pick things up once visualized.

As a common guideline, visual indicators overcome touch when people judge the external properties of an object, such as its size or shape, while tactile indicators are predominant when evaluating microstructural features of a product, such as texture or temperature (Gallace and Spence, 2011). As Howes (2005) noted, playing with a product's feel through the alteration of its tactile attributes provides an additional mean of differentiating a particular product from those of the competition. Using Apple iPod is a good example of this. In fact, according to Johnson (2007) tactile branding is a method that helps marketers plant a clear idea of a product's identity and benefit – psychological, emotional and functional – without having to use optical awareness, or oral or scent; it is strictly by touch. They want to convey a benefit and awareness and an identity by touch. Apple's personal music player is one of the most obvious examples. It is said that if we were to put 10 different MP3 players on a table, anyone who had ever owned an iPod would be able to tactfully identify the iPod.

However, our explicit association of a certain brand with a particular tactile attribute might be misleading. Gentile *et al.* (2007) conducted a study in which participants were asked to rate the sensory modality most important to them in purchasing specific products. A table of scientific criteria was produced where, for example 'Pringles' potato chips were distinctive for their taste alone, ignoring the importance of the crunch sound when biting into a chip. 'Harley-Davidson' motorcycles were considered to be desirable because of their visual aspects overlooking the impact of their distinctive roar. Lastly the iPod success was attributed to its musical clarity, but neglecting the importance of its tactile feel. The above analyses showed how important it is to pay attention to the new arising tendencies in customers' behaviour interpretation. The study proved that a relevant part of the value proposed to customers, and actually recognized by them, is linked to experiential features; we found that, regardless of the context, customers want to live positive consumption experiences. Living a positive customer experience can promote the creation of an emotional tie between a firm's brand and its customers which in turn enhance customer loyalty. This does not imply that customers neglected the importance of functionalities: sometimes as required standard, sometimes as factors enabling an optimal experience.

6.4 Conclusions

The sense of touch is one of the central forms of perceptual experience. Positive touch from others is necessary for an individual's healthy development. Often ignored when we talk about our fundamental senses, the sensation of touch is a fundamental part of our daily experience, influencing what we buy, who we love and even how we heal. We use this sense to gather information about our surroundings and as a means of establishing trust and social bonds with other people.

Vision and smell alone are not always enough for consumers to evaluate products or to make purchase decisions, and omit other important information, such as on the form, robustness, texture or weight of a product that the sense of touch (or tactile sense) might convey. Visual and tactile senses can be identified as the most active of our five senses. In retail management practice, it is obvious that the tactile sense, as a sensory channel, is significant in purchase and consumption processes for goods such as cars, computers, clothing, home equipment, mobile phones, shoes or for restaurant services.

Touching an object influences a consumer's perception of ownership and the amount they are willing to pay for an object. Touch means acquiring knowledge about the product and its characteristics, such as form, hardness, texture or weight. It has potentially significant implications for store atmospherics, in the form of in-store and point-of-purchase displays. Researchers claim that displays should encourage touch and result in an interaction with products that customers would otherwise have ignored. This could increase impulse and unplanned purchases.

Touch behaviour has been overlooked in research, despite the fact that consumers use this sense to obtain information about products and become frustrated if they are unable to touch them.

Touch is likely to offer numerous opportunities for innovative branding and marketing in the years to come. Some companies are even going further and considering the practicalities associated with trademarking the signature feel of their brands to help distinguish them from the competition at a more emotional and/or affective level.

References

Ballantine, P.W., Jack, R. and Parsons, A.G., 2010. Atmospheric cues and their effect on the hedonic retail experience. International Journal of Retail and Distribution Management 38: 641-653.

Cicero, S., 2009. The sense of touch. Available at: http://tinyurl.com/mmojl2y.

Citrin, A.V., Stem, D.E., Spangenberg, E.R. and Clark, M.J., 2003. Consumer need for tactile input: an internet retailing challenge. Journal of Business Research 56: 915-922.

Field, T., 2003. Touch. MIT Press, Cambridge, MA, USA, 200 pp.

Fiorini, F., 2015. Autotelic versus instrumental need for touch: empirical evidence from a field study, LUISS Guido Carli, Rome, Italy.

Fulkerson, M., 2011. The unity of haptic touch. Philosophical Psychology 24: 493-516.

Fulkerson, M., 2012. Touch without touching. Philosophers Imprint 12: 1-15.

Fulkerson, M., 2014a. The first sense: a philosophical study of human touch. MIT Press, Cambridge, MA, USA, 220 pp.

Fulkerson, M., 2014b. Rethinking the senses and their interactions: The case for sensory pluralism. Frontiers in Psychology 5: 1426.

Fulkerson, M., 2014c. What counts as touch? In: Stokes, D., Matthen, M. and Biggs, S. (eds.) Perception and its modalities. Oxford University Press, New York, NY, USA, pp. 191-204.

Fulkerson, M., 2016. Touch. In: Zalta, E.N. (ed.) The Stanford encyclopedia of philosophy. Stanford University, Stanford, CA, USA.

Gallace, A. and Spence, C., 2010. The science of interpersonal touch: an overview. Neuroscience and Biobehavioral Reviews 34: 246-259.

Gallace, A. and Spence, C., 2011. To what extent do gestalt grouping principles influence tactile perception? Psychological Bulletin 137: 538-561.

Gallace, A. and Spence, C., 2014. In touch with the future: the sense of touch from cognitive neuroscience to virtual reality. Oxford University Press, Oxford, UK, 469 pp.

Gentile, C., Spiller, N. and Noci, G., 2007. How to sustain the customer experience: an overview of experience components that co-create value with the customer. European Management Journal 25: 395-410.

Grohmann, B., Spangenberg, E.R. and Sprott, D.E., 2007. The influence of tactile input on the evaluation of retail product offerings. Journal of Retailing 83: 237-245.

Hatfield, R.W., 1994. Touch and human sexuality. In: Bullough, V.L., Bullough, B. and Stein, A. (eds.) Human sexuality: an encyclopedia. Garland Publishing, New York, NY, USA.

Howes, D., 2005. Empire of the senses: the sensual culture reader. Bloomsbury Publishing, New York, NY, USA, 432 pp.

Hultén, B., 2012. Sensory cues and shoppers' touching behaviour: the case of IKEA. International Journal of Retail and Distribution Management 40: 273-289.

Johnson, A., 2007. Tactile branding leads us by our fingertips. Available at: http://tinyurl.com/mlhg5xu.

Klatzky, R.L. and Lederman, S.J., 1992. Stages of manual exploration in haptic object identification. Perception and Psychophysics 52: 661-670.

Klatzky, R.L. and Lederman, S.J., 1993. Toward a computational model of constraint-driven exploration and haptic object identification. Perception 22: 597-621.

Krishna, A., 2012. An integrative review of sensory marketing: engaging the senses to affect perception, judgment and behavior. Journal of Consumer Psychology 22: 332-351.

Krishna, A. and Morrin, M., 2008. Does touch affect taste? The perceptual transfer of product container haptic cues. Journal of Consumer Research 34: 807-818.

Leonard, C., 2009. The sense of touch and how it affects development Crystal Leonard's blog. Serendip studio. Available at: http://tinyurl.com/m9fas8j.

Linden, D.J., 2016. Touch: the science of hand, heart, and mind. Penguin Books, London, UK, 272 pp.

Lindstrom, M., 2005. Brand sense: how to build powerful brands through touch, taste, smell, sight and sound. Kogan Page, London, UK, 256 pp.

Löken, L.S., Wessberg, J., Morrison, I., McGlone, F. and Olausson, H., 2009. Coding of pleasant touch by unmyelinated afferents in humans. Nature Neuroscience 12: 547-548.

McCabe, D.B. and Nowlis, S.M., 2003. The effect of examining actual products or product descriptions on consumer preference. Journal of Consumer Psychology 13: 431-439.

McGlone, F., Olausson, H., Boyle, J.A., Jones-Gotman, M., Dancer, C., Guest, S. and Essick, G., 2012. Touching and feeling: differences in pleasant touch processing between glabrous and hairy skin in humans. European Journal of Neuroscience 35: 1782-1788.

Möller, J. and Herm, S., 2013. Shaping retail brand personality perceptions by bodily experiences. Journal of Retailing 89: 438-446.

Montagu, A., 1971. Touching: the human significance of the skin. Columbia University Press, Oxford, UK, 494 pp.

Noad, J. and Rogers, B., 2008. The importance of retail atmospherics in B2B retailing: the case of BOC. International Journal of Retail and Distribution Management 36: 1002-1014.

Peck, J. and Childers, T.L., 2003. To have and to hold: the influence of haptic information on product judgments. Journal of Marketing 67: 35-48.

Peck, J. and Johnson, J.W., 2011. Autotelic need for touch, haptics, and persuasion: the role of involvement. Psychology and Marketing 28: 222-239.

Peck, J. and Shu, S.B., 2009. The effect of mere touch on perceived ownership. Journal of Consumer Research 36: 434-447.

Peck, J. and Wiggins, J., 2006. It just feels good: customers' affective response to touch and its influence on persuasion. Journal of Marketing 70: 56-69.

Shu, S.B. and Peck, J., 2011. Psychological ownership and affective reaction: emotional attachment process variables and the endowment effect. Journal of Consumer Psychology 21: 439-452.

Soars, B., 2009. Driving sales through shoppers' sense of sound, sight, smell and touch. International Journal of Retail and Distribution Management 37: 286-298.

Spence, C. and Gallace, A., 2011. Multisensory design: reaching out to touch the consumer. Psychology and Marketing 28: 267-308.

Spence, C., Puccinelli, N.M., Grewal, D. and Roggeveen, A.L., 2014. Store atmospherics: a multisensory perspective. Psychology and Marketing 31: 472-488.

Printed in the United States
by Baker & Taylor Publisher Services